MW01199165

Leitourgia Press

Reviews

"Dr. Heck's Journey is not only a moving account of one man's pursuit of truth, but a rich reflection on Christian faith that will stir anyone who is willing to step into the beautiful world Tim opens up to us. In a gentle and accessible way, Dr. Heck provides theologically rich accounts of various points of Catholic faith and practice that were important in his path. Without an ounce of pressure to agree with him, he offers these points along with thoughtful questions at the end of each chapter to make us think about our own faith and personal journey. I highly recommend this book to anyone who wants to see evidence of God's work in the human heart, and especially to anyone who wants to know how to let Him work in his or her own heart."

-Fr. Boniface Hicks, OSB
Director of Spiritual Formation and the Institute
for Ministry Formation
Saint Vincent Seminary, Latrobe, PA

"St. Paul told the church of Thessalonica that 'so deeply do we care for you that we are determined to share with you not only the gospel of God but our own selves.' Dr. Tim Heck has shared with the reader not simply a story of conversion but his own heart and the cost of following the Lamb wherever he goes. As a friend, he offers gentle guidance through thoughtful questions, allowing space for the Lord to speak as he wants. This work is a gift to those just beginning, those along the way, and those who already enjoy the full communion of the Catholic Church yet perhaps have come to take it for granted. May this book be a help to each of its readers, wherever they are on the journey."

-Fr. James Baron, S.T.L.

"Making that personal decision to be a follower of Jesus Christ can truly be seen as a death and resurrection experience. At some point in our search for truth, we ultimately die to our way of thinking and embrace the reality that Jesus is who He says He is. That there is a God! (And as a reminder, it's not me!!) *My Journey of Faith* is Tim Heck's humble reckoning that he might not be right about the truth of the Church founded by Jesus Himself 2,000 years ago. His Protestant upbringing had shrouded his faith journey in misunderstandings and confusion about the Catholic Church and what she claims to be. For Catholics, Tim's personal journey is a reminder of why we are Catholic. For Catholic converts, the tale walks us back into the adventure of those days we decided the truth about Jesus was, in fact, rooted in His Church. For non-Catholics, a word of caution – if you are open to the possibility the Catholic Church is what she claims to be, this book might change your life."

-Chuck Neff
TV and Radio Broadcaster and Producer

"The details of Tim's life and experience from his childhood and family that traces his life history of the faith to the present are both endearing and genuine. The pages of this book teach and evangelize the beauty and truth of the Catholic faith. His words and genuine story are easily relatable and will open the hearts, ears, and minds of readers."

-Kimlarie Lloyd
Customer Service Manager
Homeschool Connections PA

"What I remember is meeting weekly with a gentleman who strenuously wrestled with the sheer insanity of coming to terms with the Catholic faith and with entering the Catholic Church. In reading this book, Tim's parents, family, pastors, professors, and friends are all very active in leading him into his belief in and love for Jesus Christ and in serving Him. Tim of all people knows the wrenching pain and suffering required to shatter that heart of stone."

-Marcus Woods
Tim's RCIA Sponsor

"Dr. Tim Heck has been "equip[ing] the saints for the work of ministry, for building up the body of Christ" for his whole life. His conversion story displays the working of the Holy Spirit in Tim's life as he undertook the work of ministry first as an ordained pastor and now in full communion with the Catholic Church. This little gem of a book should see wide distribution in RCIA courses and among those interested in engaging in the exploration of the claims of the Catholic Church to be the body of Christ at work here and now."

-Will Riley, J.D.
RileyCate, LLC

"Through Tim's search for truth, his theological struggles, sacrifices, and even the pains of transitioning between two different Christian worlds, there is an inspiring story of conversion, surrender, and trust. And at the center of it all, the Holy Eucharist. We need to hear more stories like Tim's."

-Rev. Kirk J. Slattery
Pastor, St. Gabriel's Catholic Church
Colorado Springs, Colorado

"From the moment I was born my dad taught me to know and love God. Little did we know he was following the very first teaching in the Catechism of The Catholic Church. I didn't become Catholic because my dad had converted but when the scales were removed from my eyes and I recognized Jesus in The Catholic Church, the first person I wanted to tell was my dad. He was there when I received my First Communion and for each of my children's sacraments thus far. I am especially grateful he has put his conversion story to paper so that my children will always know how brave their grandfather was to risk everything for The Truth."

"The truth is like a lion; you don't have to defend it. Let it loose and it will defend itself." St. Augustine

Jessica McCaffrey
Tim's daughter, Wife of Ryan, Mother of Six

"As a practicing cradle Catholic, I found Tim's journey from Evangelical Protestantism to the Catholic church to be inspiring. It serves as a good reminder that God is patient and will never stop pursuing our hearts. Keep asking questions and going deeper into the faith!"

- Therese Basgell
Catholic wife and mother

My Journey of Faith

WHY I LEFT THE PROTESTANT
EVANGELICAL WORLD FOR *ROME*

Timothy Heck, PhD.

Leitourgia Press
Colorado Springs, Colorado

Author: **Timothy Heck**
Publisher: **Leitourgia Press**
Edited by **Therese Basgall**

www.leitourgiapress.com

Book Layout ©2017 BookDesignTemplates.com
Cover Photo by **Shane Rodimel Photography**

My Journey of Faith/ Timothy Heck. —1st ed.
ISBN 978-1-0880-9651-2
Library of Congress Control Number: 2023935908

Contents

Dedicated to my brother Gary,
whose friendship I miss dearly.

GARY CHARLES HECK

1953-2022

"To become a Catholic is not to leave off thinking, but to learn how to think."

—G. K. CHESTERTON

Acknowledgements

I am grateful to so many who made this *journey* possible in my life. It would not be possible to list the names of all the people who provided me the nourishment and guidance needed to make this trek, but there are a few for whom I will be eternally grateful. It was Marcus who launched me down this *westward* road and then sponsored me as I was received into the Catholic Church on Easter Vigil, 2003 and I cannot thank him enough. Though we have spoken only on a few occasions, Dr. Scott Hahn has been my mentor through his writings and his lectures. I thank God there are those who can articulate theology so compellingly. For Therese being willing to lend her literary skills in the editing of this personal journal, I am grateful. And for my beloved Margie who tolerated my struggles throughout those most challenging years before we together received our First Eucharist, you will always be my *karis* graced to me from above.

Motivations for Telling My Story

It has been almost twenty years since I was blessed with those Holy Oils of Sacramental Confirmation, but the sweet fragrance lingers on. At times it seems a lifetime ago that this journey took such an unexpected turn toward *Rome* and the Catholic Church. Sadly, there was a time I couldn't use those three words in conversation or print except in a context of disdaining condemnation. Today they remind me who I am as a chosen child of God received into his family with a history two millennia old.

Usually, the question comes when someone sees the Crucifix hanging from my neck or sees me making the Sign of the Cross as I bow to pray over my meal or reads through my professional Disclosure Statement as a mental health therapist and sees that I am Catholic. It sounds something like this, spoken with staccato surprise—*"You're Catholic!?"* Not so well hidden inside the question is the intrigue of how I could remain in such an archaic religious institution, given the countless alternatives that offer so much more contemporary vibrancy. You can only imagine their chagrin when I tell them I converted from Protestant Evangelical Christianity to the Catholic Church.

Over the years I have observed that converts like me, that is, those who may have been raised in the Evangelical Christian community, called to ministry in a Protestant Christian Church, educated formally in Seminary and even Ordained to the Pastoral Ministry, find it helpful, and maybe even necessary, to offer a defense for their decision to convert. My psychotherapy background leads me to see it as the fulfillment of a psychological need to make sense out of such a drastic life course change. After all, there are not a few people who still consider coming into the Catholic

Church to be a radical act of sacrilegious heresy. Of course, most people won't give voice to those thoughts, though I did have one acquaintance say outright to me, *"I thought the Catholic Church was the whore of Babylon."*, to which I found myself stupefied that anyone could still accept such a judgment proposed by some narrow fundamentalists who have likely never dared to open the pages of the Catechism of the Catholic Church, speak to a Catholic Priest, let alone step inside the door of a Catholic Parish to investigate their false assumptions.

So, why am I choosing to tell my own story of conversion after all these years? Well, I do still get asked the obvious question, though typically in much kinder fashion, *"Why?"* St. Peter does admonish us to always be ready with an answer when asked to give a defense of our faith (1 Peter 3:15). Maybe I'm overdue to offer my own explanation as a defense of one of, if not the most, serious decisions of my life.

But hopefully my motivation for writing is deeper than the satisfaction of an egotistical need to justify what might seem to many as a foolish act or a random choice for some personal benefit. Further, if I believe what I claim to believe every time I recite the Nicene or Apostles Creed, and I very much do, then I am compelled to share the truth afforded to me in this journey. Perhaps the Holy Spirit will use my story to encourage or lead you to the next step in your own journey of faith.

> *"But sanctify Christ as Lord in your hearts. Always be ready to give an explanation to anyone who asks you for a reason for your hope, but do it with gentleness and reverence, keeping your conscience clear."*
>
> I Peter 3:15

Let me encourage you to pass this little book along to someone else after you read it. Or maybe leave it out on a coffee table where it might be noticed. Even if your visitors and guests don't read it, it might stir up a question in their own minds about this journey we all are making of our lives. I have purposely kept the chapters brief so you can read a chapter a day in less than ten minutes or work your way through the whole book in about an hour.

At the end of each chapter, I have included a few questions to prime the pump on your own story. Whether you are Catholic, Protestant, a "non" or even an agnostic, it is never a bad thing to ponder the deeper questions of life and our existence in this world and the world to come.

CHAPTER ONE

Raised in a Christian World

My parents were devout Christians with a clear conviction of the priority of God. It was a faith demonstrated in not just weekly, but daily observance of the practice. We wouldn't dare take a bite of food at a meal without first bowing our heads and offering a prayer of thanks. Their friends were generally part of our Church community. Attending Youth Group, Sunday School, annual Church Camp were all considered just part of being in our family. If they were Catholic, they would likely have been daily communicants and at least weekly adorers at the Blessed Sacrament. But they were not Catholic. In fact, they were thoroughly Bible-believing, evangelical, Protestants who would refer to the Catholic Church in a disparaging way that could only be interpreted as a sad judgment on an ignorant religion that lost its way from the days of the Apostles.

The congregation where we worshiped was in downtown Indianapolis. As a child I thought it had to be the largest and most austere edifice ever built. The ceilings were over 50 feet high with a baptistry placed precisely in the center of the front wall behind and above the pulpit and Communion Table. The organ's pipes were masked behind a thin veil that maintained a clean sharp appearance where the robed choir elegantly led the assembly in grand hymns that were as known to me as the folks tunes of James Taylor, John Denver, and the likes of Harry Chapin, I had come to love.

Dad served in about every capacity there was, always leading with his strong gifts, talents, and humble character. He was an incredible artist, an avid reader and had a flair for presentation. Many years he served as the leader of the Junior Worship experience where children of all ages gathered in a chapel to sing, pray, and hear him speak, as well as other leaders in the church. Sometimes they called it Junior Church. Sounds a bit odd these days as I contemplate my current understanding of worship, but it made good sense in that context as the children were being taught how to do what any good Evangelical would consider worship. That included singing with fervor, praying attentively, and listening respectfully to the teaching of the minister from the pulpit.

Sunday mornings consisted of Worship and Sunday School, or sometimes those same two elements in reverse. The school part of the experience was age focused from nursery to adults and all the way to the elder generation. Dad was, of course, a teacher of one of the adult classes and always did an excellent job keeping people's attention with his creative use of teaching tools and visuals. Mother attended a women's class where she enjoyed many friendships that remained close to her even to her death at 96 years of age this year. Our denomination had its own publishing houses, so we had access to curriculum for all grade levels that would match any public-school secular curriculum with its expert quality and design.

Worship usually was a 60–90-minute service that was quite reverent, formal, and even liturgical, though we would never have used such an obviously *religious* and seemingly *Catholic* description for what we were doing in the setting of worship. From the stained glass to the baptistry to the Communion Table and the

pews, everything about the experience resembled an ancient practice I would one day discover to be liturgy.

Englewood Christian Church in Indianapolis, Indiana where Tim was baptized.

cover to be liturgy. Dad served as a Deacon and then later an Elder. In my youth I always saw it in a hierarchical fashion, and it appeared he moved up in his ecclesial career to the office of Elder and for years he served as the Chairman of the Elders. The truth is, that would be approximate to the role of the Bishop in the Catholic Church, but our leaders were very careful about the terminology used throughout the faith. I later came to see there was much arbitrary discrimination and license taken with this linguistic process.

We dressed up to go to Church, which for me meant dress pants, collared shirt, tie, and jacket, with my shoes nicely shined, a ritual Dad and I carried out faithfully before we left the house Sunday mornings. He was my model, mentor, and hero, all wrapped up in a man who influenced my life more than any other individual. And I miss him dearly since he passed nine years before this writing. As a now practicing Catholic, I have a close relationship with him through my prayers for him during the Eucharistic Prayer at Mass and as I request that he pray on my behalf.

My two older brothers were also faithful in their observance of our Christian faith. In fact, Gary attended a Bible College (the same one I would attend two years after him) and was ordained to the Christian Ministry upon his graduation, subsequently serving on the staff of several Christian Churches around the country. Steve did not go into formal ministry, but his career in secular education prepared him to be a strong student of the Word and always very active in the leadership of the local congregation where he and his family were members. My younger sister of ten years attended a Christian Liberal Arts College and has also lived out her Christian faith beautifully throughout her life.

Suffice to say, I was raised in a distinctively Christian world and let me add, my conversion to the Catholic Church in no way should be seen as a declaration of nullity as to the validity of that catechetical culture that trained me, formed me, and motivated me to always seek God in my life. It was precisely because I was skilled in my study of the Bible and theology, inspired by the passionate spirituality of my family, and challenged by that background, that I continued to study and search for the fulness of the truth, which I eventually found in the Catholic Church.

Please indulge me for a few more moments as I share a couple stories with you from my early years on this journey of faith. The first was in the Spring of 1966 when I came to a personal conviction that Jesus was not only the Lord and Christ of whom the prophets had written, but that I wanted him to be my personal Savior and Lord. For us, that meant I might be ready for baptism. Like Catholics, we took seriously the teachings of our Lord that we must be discipled in the faith, catechized in the Word, and formed in the mind to be ready for conversion and reception of the

Sacraments. While we did not use the term, *Sacrament*, to describe baptism, we did take a sacramental perspective on the symbol, believing it was an essential part of the conversion experience and should only be undertaken when one has the mental capacity to understand and acknowledge one's sinfulness, a willingness to repent and a desire for salvation through Christ's sacrifice on the cross. That is just what happened after Dick Laue, our Senior Minister at Englewood Christian Church, came to our home and walked me through all the scrutinies of the faith, which I passed with flying colors, not surprisingly since my parents had taught me so well. So, at the age of ten, I was immersed in Christian baptism for the forgiveness of my sins, in the Name of the Father, Son and Holy Spirit. Yes, our tradition practiced full immersion, not only because it was more in keeping with the first century practice of the early Church, but because it more beautifully symbolized the passive posture of reception of the grace bestowed upon us in baptism. Like any of the Sacraments, we do not take them, rather we receive them.

The second story I want to share is when I was in Junior High, perhaps thirteen or fourteen, and I participated in what was called "The Pentecost Speech Contest" at our church. Gary and I shared in that experience several years straight and were usually in the top three finish positions, proudly. But one year stands out for me, when I memorized the 17th chapter of Acts, which is St. Paul's address to the Athenians in the Areopagus. In full theatrical fashion I then recited the entire chapter to the audience assembled for the event. It wasn't just a performance though, it was a convicting incident that showed me my ability to speak articulately, move a listening audience, and even more, be a spokesperson for the Lord. Though I am no longer an Ordained Christian Minister, I remain committed to being a **spokesperson** for God, regardless of the setting or audience.

Questions to Consider

1. Who introduced you to Jesus Christ and what was that encounter like for you?

2. What were you taught about the role and place of the Church in your early time of being discipled in the Christian faith?

3. Did your early experience in the faith inspire you to want to increase your own understanding of Christianity?

CHAPTER TWO

Educated in a Restoration Theology

T he faith tradition of Christianity in which I was raised was part of the 19th century Restoration Movement out of which three mainstreams of the church emerged. Like any Protestant culture, division is always not far removed from the initial revival. The first breach coincided with our nation's Civil War and coincidentally that division took place along the Mason-Dixon Line that separated the North from the South. The second split was about 50 years later, leaving this once powerful revival now splintered into three separate branches, each vying for the authority of truth.

The founders of the Movement were men of great wisdom and theological learning: Thomas and Alexander Campbell, Walter Scott, Barton Stone, and many others. During my years at a Christian college and then later at Seminary, I found reading the debates of these scholars quite informing and stimulating. Like great warriors in battle, they wielded their weaponry expertly. I came to respect them and see them as our own "Early Fathers of the Faith", whose desire was to restore the Christian faith to its original New Testament beauty.

The pioneers of this fast-growing movement held to a few fundamental principles. The first was consistent with their Reformation ancestry, a strong appeal to the Scriptures as the sole source of Divine truth and the basis for all Christian belief and practice, that is, the New Testament. This was expressed in several slogans that became characteristic of its seminarians and congregational adherents.

*Where the Bible speaks, we
speak, where the Bible is silent,
we are silent.*[1]

*We are not the only Christians,
but we are Christians only.*[2]

Such statements as these were our battle-cries around which we gathered and found a strong sense of solidarity. We were admonished to study these great orators and their writings with a confidence that they were interpreting the Word of God with a precision that mirrored what I would one day understand as the Magisterium of the Church. However, this was just a band of well-intentioned believers who were on a diligent search for the truth and sincerely thought they had discovered gold.

I'll never forget calling one of my respected Professors from Seminary during my studies of Catholicism and his only words to me were, *"Tim, stop reading the early Church fathers and read the Reformers."* When I questioned the sheer illogic and unreasonableness of

---

[1] Thomas Campbell
[2] Unknown source

such a limited approach to the deepest questions of ecclesiology, he cut off the conversation and we never spoke again. That was a sad, but very common pattern I came to experience with my former instructors and friends.

Cincinnati Bible Seminary Library in Ohio

Most of us may recall playing that silly game in our younger days called **Telephone**. Everyone sits in a circle and one person in the circle begins by telling the person sitting on one side of her a story. Then that person turns to the person on their other side and tells him the same story and on it goes on until it circles back to the original person. Finally, the last person tells the story as they heard it, the story having now traveled around the circle. What he shares is usually considerably different from the original tale. Not only is it an excellent way to reveal the inherent problems with gossip, but it also provides a strong principle about the origins of truth.

Ironically, the well-intentioned reformers of the Restoration Movement were incredibly deliberate about going back to the story of the faith as found in the New Testament, however they stopped at the end of the Apostolic age, that is, with the death of the last Apostle of Jesus. Their reasoning was that those who followed the original Apostles and authors of Scripture were not inspired by the Holy Spirit and so their testimony is not trustworthy. Well, I wouldn't challenge that logic, but I also wouldn't assume all non-inspired testimony to be untrustworthy. Think about it this way—mathematical truths are not explicitly found within the pages of inspired Scripture, yet they are trustworthy. My doctoral program introduced me to the scientific method of arriving at truth and validating those findings. Naturally, we always have a margin of error, that percentage of chance that our findings were just that, a product of chance. But this merely means that there are degrees of trustworthiness.

Like other similar Christian Movements seeking to recover the early vibrancy of the faith, we should applaud these 19th century *restorers*. Yet there is no need to dismiss altogether the continued practice of the faith that followed the first century age and throughout the subsequent eighteen centuries. Granted, there were heresies, apostasies, and doctrinal distortions that occurred over those years, and they warrant close examination to draw the truth out of the often-hypocritical practices. Still, like our *Telephone* game, there are always elements of truth even in the last person's recounting of the original.

What's my point? Read, study, and examine the understanding of those early believers who were evangelized and discipled by the Apostles themselves and then continue that exploration over the subsequent centuries. These extant writings are referred to, of course, as the early Church fathers. When my own study of ecclesiastical history led me to read many of these writings, it was remarkable how closely they resembled not only the theology, but the liturgical practice of the Catholic Church.

This is probably a good time for that oft-quoted statement of the highly respected convert from the Anglican Church, Cardinal John Henry Newman, *"To be deep in history is to cease to be a Protestant"*. Not everyone who studies the history of Christianity will convert to the Catholic Church, but a serious read of the life, doctrine, and liturgical practices of the early Christians over those first six centuries will at least create some healthy, though possibly bewildering, dissonance.

Questions to Consider

1. Think about the Church or Denomination you are affiliated with and consider why you chose it as your community of faith. What were your motivations and rationale?

2. What did you discover about the origin and history of your Church or Denomination when you explored it?

3. How confident are you that your Church or Denomination is practicing the fullness of the Christian faith? What is the source of your confidence?

4. If you have not researched the background of your Church affiliation, consider what keeps you from these challenging questions?

CHAPTER THREE

Confounded by Contradictions

hose who know me well characterize me as a bit of a perfectionist. Of course, that means I like to have everything in its place, which can make me a nuisance to my wife at times and much too particular when working on a project. It also means I struggle with inconsistencies in life. During my years in Bible College and Seminary I encountered many inconsistencies and contradictions. Searching for answers was a never-ending and yet somewhat of an elusive journey that motivated me to study and ask difficult questions of my instructors.

Systematic Theology was one of my favorite courses as it attempts to define categorically the Christian faith. That was appealing to me, but it still didn't resolve all the confusion. The professor leaned toward a Reformed theology, which meant that he was a huge fan of John Calvin, the one who articulately gave more theological substance to Luther's reform effort, the latter being more of the evangelist with a new dream. Sadly, it was a dream that would lead to a fracture in the Church that has only continued to fracture over the past five-hundred years. Despite my professor's intricately organized doctrinal course, the contradictions were not resolved.

> *Systematic Theology was one of my favorite courses as it attempts to define categorically the Christian faith.*

How can the community our Lord founded before he ascended into heaven fragment into a disintegrated institution with literally thousands, even tens of thousands, of branches each vying for exclusivity as the one true Church he left here on earth? The theology of the Church I had studied in Seminary did not match the practical ecclesiology of Christendom I encountered after graduation and ordination. Where could I find the One, True Church in the 20th century? The answer I was given in my Protestant tradition said that church is only found in the *spiritual* realm, not the practical one of reality in which we live.

This proposed solution to the visible problem of Christianity's splintered condition would suffice to a point. After all, we live in a fallen world, so how could we expect anything more? Yet I wanted more, much more, and my deepest inclinations were to doubt the validity of this position. After all, this isn't a man-made organization, but a family in which God the Father, Son and Holy Spirit is the head. I expected more than what I was exposed to and I, as a Minister of the Gospel of Jesus Christ, needed more than what I was given if I was to effectively represent our Lord in my pastoral role.

What are we to do when we encounter problems and contradictions around our faith? I fell back on the belief that there were answers to my dilemmas and deposited the difficulty with me, not God. In other words, I blamed myself for not being able to figure it out, for being too naïve to understand the answers my mentors and professors had given me, or perhaps I just did not have sufficient faith to accept the truth of Christianity when it came to these ecclesial matters.

This is where my graduate work in Psychology played a strong role in my search. The scientific method of discovering truth begins with the identification of a problem. From there the researcher proposes some possible hypotheses for consideration and exploration. A study is conducted, and the data is gathered. After careful analysis, interpretations and implications are rendered, adding to the body of knowledge around the subject. Up to this point in my life I was operating under numerous assumptions that could not be supported by serious research, such as:

- *The Restoration Movement discovered all the truths of the Christian faith that had been hidden for some 18 centuries.*

- *A religious institution or denomination could never represent the original community Christ established in the first century, instead believing every local congregation is autonomous and self-governing.*

- *And the existence of moral corruption negates the possibility of the Church's theological integrity.*

This list is not meant to be exhaustive, just to serve as examples to better understand the concerns I encountered as I studied ecclesiology[3].

Science, even the *softer* science of Psychology, tends to make skeptics out of its adherents. Indeed, part of me was engulfed in such skepticism, but I always managed to bury it beneath a mound of activity and an appearance of clarity. And what would be gained, or so I thought to myself, by admitting to these concerns? It would only bring my credibility into question with the very people to whom I was trying to minister and whose faith I so wanted to deepen.

In the early 90s I began my clinical work as a Marriage and Family Therapist and had the privilege of working in both hospital and outpatient settings. By 1993, with the strong encouragement of Gary Rowe, one of my very good friends from college and seminary days who was now a Pastoral Counselor on the staff of the largest Christian Church in Indianapolis, I launched my own Private Practice. Initially, my office was housed in a small church who welcomed my presence as a professional ministry for the community that

---

[3] Theology, as applied to the nature and study of the Christian Church.

might also introduce people to faith when they enter the walls of the Church. In the coming year Gary would appeal to me to take on some of his Interns who were preparing for licensure in the field. With some reluctance, as I never considered myself a strong Clinical Supervisor, I began to work with one and then another and another, until my Private Practice had become a very successful Group Practice.

Gary Rowe

It was very rewarding to offer my limited expertise to help people who were struggling. Admittedly, the counseling work got off to a slow start in those early months. One day, with many more hours available than filled with clients, I took to my knees and prayed God would give me direction about the work, questioning him about how to proceed. The voice was not audible, but I sensed without a doubt the message and was convinced the source was from above. In essence, the Lord said to me, *"Tim, work from your own struggles, failures, and brokenness."* That meant I would specialize my work and focus on three kinds of problems in my work as a licensed therapist, *anxiety, depression,* and *marriage.*

Instead of treating anyone who called for help, I started taking only cases that fell into one of these three categories. I understood anxiety and depression from my adolescent years forward. Going into the field of Psychotherapy gave me hope of finding some answers. Like anyone else who enters this profession, I soon learned the answers would be less about cure and more about coping. As for marriage, my own failed marriage was a school of suffering in which I painfully came to understand first-hand the dynamic principles studied in graduate school.

Questions to Consider

1. Reading a chapter like this one might lead to some cognitive dissonance, that is, a sense of confusion that the matters of faith are not as clear as we might have thought them to be. Does that at all resonate with your reaction to what you just read?

2. When you encounter some of the seeming contradictions in your faith, the Scriptures, or the Church, how do you respond and what do you do to try and resolve them?

3. Think about the last conversation you had with someone who was a committed Christian but belonged to a Church that you are confident is not holding to a Biblically sound set of doctrines. How did that affect your way of thinking about the faith?

4. At times in history, most recently in the late 19th and through the mid 20th centuries, doctrinal differences were attempted to be resolved through public debates. It is arguable just how effective they were, but would you attend such an event, and do you think you would be open to hearing views presented by someone who held beliefs contrary to your own in matters of faith?

CHAPTER FOUR

Encounter with an Informed and Formed Catholic

I f you asked me in my twenties whether I was open-minded I would have given you a strong affirmative answer. "Absolutely I am open to hearing other points of view, contrary perceptions, examining the evidence someone might put forth who has reached conclusions different than my own!" Truth be known, I was not. My mind had been indoctrinated by well-intentioned parents, pastors, youth group leaders, Sunday School teachers, and even professors who had little appreciation for historic Christianity prior to the sixteenth century and the Protestant Reformers.

When it came to Catholics, I had relegated them to a category of uninformed followers being led astray by a corrupt clergy who had no regard for the Word of God and virtually no real understanding of its teachings. Most closed-minded people are also judgmental, and I was no exception. It was also easy for me to disregard Catholicism, never even considering it a remote competition for the true faith of Christianity. That is, until Marcus showed up in my office.[4]

If a person's church affiliation came up in conversation and they told me they were Catholic, my general attitude was that they were not Christian at all and were prime targets for an evangelistic encounter. Sometimes a door seemed to *open* and I would share tidbits about God, His love for us and maybe even encourage the person to seek out a church to attend. Many evangelicals have been trained in some version

---

[4] Marcus has given me permission to disclose his story and our first meeting in a professional setting. To avoid a dual relationship, it was months following the termination of our work together that I reached back out to him with my questions about the Catholic Church.

of *friendship evangelism* wherein the goal is to establish a relationship of friendship and then begin to bring the person to Jesus Christ as the ultimate goal.

Steubenville is in northeast Ohio on the Ohio River at the intersection of West Virginia, Ohio, and Pennsylvania, less than an hour from Pittsburgh. Other than its geographical proximity to Pittsburgh, just across the river, it might escape notice were it not for the Franciscan University in the heart of the small town. Not exactly a paradise setting, unless you are looking for a community of devout Catholic faithful, impressive Christian scholarship, and a powerful manifestation of the Holy Spirit. Marcus had earned his Master of Arts in Theology from the well-respected Franciscan University that emerged out of the charismatic movement that swept through much of Christendom, including Catholicism, in the '70s. What astounded me as much as this young man's knowledge of Christianity was his pious devotion to living out his faith and sharing it with others, as he would do with me in the months that followed our encounter.

The tutelage began with a series of twelve cassette tapes (this was the late '90s) in a binder for a course he had taken at the college entitled *A Refutation of*

Sola Scriptura by **Dr. Scott Hahn**. Here was my plan—pop the first tape into my car audio, listen to it for five minutes, pull it out and when Marcus asked me about it, I would be able to say, with a livable measure of integrity, that I had listened to

Dr. Scott Hahn

some of it and appreciated the gesture. After all, I knew the Reformation principles and could manage an apologetic for reliance on the Scriptures alone without having to hear this lecturer drone on about it.

Looking back, I think my expectation was that we would bow out of this difficult and potentially tense dialogue with a mutual respect for the other's position on matters of Christian faith and that would be the end of it. The plan was obliterated when I quickly discovered this professor[5] was not only an incredibly studied scholar, but a penetrating teacher who could articulate his thoughts and defend his positions with precision. Furthermore, he had been a Protestant Minister,

---

[5] Dr. Scott Hahn is an American Catholic theologian and Christian apologist. A former Presbyterian who converted to Catholicism, Hahn's popular works include Rome Sweet Home and The Lamb's Supper: The Mass as Heaven on Earth.

rather vehement in his anti-Catholic sentiment, only to convert to the Catholic Church. Suffice to say, I was in trouble.

The first time hearing these lectures I was struck by his arguments and even more so by my inability to develop a reasonable response in defense of my long-held belief in the *formal principle* of the Reformers known as *sola scriptura*. Interestingly, I did not hold to the parallel *material principle* of that 16th century movement known as *sola fide*, meaning "through faith alone". This would become key in my conversion to the Catholic Church later when I wrestled with the theology of works in our salvation. By the third time of working through this recorded course I was sitting at my desk, taking notes, writing down sources and preparing to delve into a stream that would drown me in the fulness of the truth about Christianity.

Since Marcus was seeing me for help with some personal issues, I determined not to engage him on these matters of faith at the time and instead, put them on a back burner so as not to interfere with our work. But little did he know that he had lit a spark in me and prompted me to begin a journey from which I could not be deterred, reading book after book about

Catholicism, its history, theology, ecclesiology, and more. My appetite was growing steadily, and I needed someone to guide me in this search.

Eventually my professional relationship with Marcus came to an end and he went on his way. The hope was that I would find someone as informed and passionate as he was who could help me with my questions. Unfortunately, that person never presented, and I was not able to make this journey on my own. The books were piling up, along with the questions, and I needed someone to talk them through.

Several months following the end of my work with Marcus, I discernably decided to reach back out to him and inquire if he would be open to meeting for a cup of coffee and talking through the course tape-series he had loaned me when we first met. He was eager to meet and came prepared to that first *java talk* loaded with books, resources, and answers. This would be the first of many such gatherings.

Questions to Consider

1. If you are a Protestant Evangelical reading this book, may I ask you to think about your view of Catholics? If you are a Catholic, may I ask you to think about how your non-Catholic friends might understand our faith through the lens of your model?

2. Have you ever talked with someone about your faith? What happened? If not, what is holding you back?

3. Suppose one of your friends asked you to explain why you are Catholic or why you are a member of your Church? What defense would you give?

4. Dr. Scott Hahn founded the St. Paul Center, a non-profit organization providing Bible Studies and countless resources for us to learn and grow in our Catholic faith. Would you take a few minutes to explore it and note what course sounds appealing to you?

CHAPTER FIVE

Faced with Obstacles

Making the decision to leave the Evangelical world of Christianity to become a Roman Catholic was not without its obstacles. They came in a variety of forms, some predictable and others quite surprising. I knew my family would have a difficult time accepting this journey. They raised their children in a church they believed held the truth, a truth that stood in striking contrast to what they knew about Catholicism.

My Mother decided she could hear me out about this crazy idea and quickly change my mind with a few well played criticisms based more on perception than reality. My Father was slightly more direct and less discrete. A strong student and teacher of the Bible himself, he was not to be bothered with any religion that seemed to add their own doctrines to those found in the Scriptures. His incredulous question to me in a tone laced with frustration spoke volumes and struck squarely on the key issue when he asked me, *"You don't believe their communion to be the actual Body and Blood of Jesus, do you!?"* In that awesome moment I came to the realization that was precisely what I had come to believe and embrace.

Tim's parents, Katie and Chuck Heck

Over time they came to see that my wife, Margie, and I were still Christians and maybe their fears were not altogether well founded. In fact, they even attended our son's Confirmation a few years later at the Parish. In our next chapter I will focus more on the psychological issues triggered when a family member makes such a drastic shift in his religious affiliation but let me just say that these can be terribly distressing for parents who have tried to raise their children in a religious belief system and were always believing and probably praying they would endure in that faith.

Many of the obstacles were doctrinal in nature. Catholic theology is undoubtedly different and sometimes in stark contrast to Protestant Evangelical Christianity. This book is not meant to be a theological treatise in defense of Catholicism as much as a personal story, so let me just identify the greatest obstacles I had to overcome in my quest for truth.

The place of **works** in the plan of salvation was one of the first obstacles to address. My history was much more in association with the radical reformers than the original reformers, which meant that I was educated to believe it would be possible to fall from grace and separate oneself from fellowship with God. Still, I would now have to deal with this issue more seriously and reconcile myself to a sanctifying lifetime process without which I could find salvation in jeopardy.

And speaking of sanctification, the place of the **Saints** in the life of the Church and growth in faith was challenging. We focused more on the present ways to understand and apply the truths of Scripture and didn't give much attention to what happened after death, assuming the one who has accepted Jesus as Savior and Lord would automatically be taken up into the heavenly realm.

On the heels of the Communion of the Saints was **purgatory** and that would require me to consider the Deutero-Canonical books of the Old Testament that were considered non-Biblical by the Reformers. And that pushed against the question of how the canon or list of the Old and New Testament books came to be developed and accepted, given that there were numerous texts that had to be discriminated in that effort.

It was like a game of Dominoes in which one doctrine fell against another and another and another. My ecclesial structure that had secured me in my faith for nearly four decades was crumbling before my eyes. Then came the matter of **baptism**. In my tradition we practiced *believer's baptism* by *immersion* because it was the individual who had to  make the decision for conversion, not the parents or anyone else. But how could I explain the early expansion of the Church traced by St. Luke in the pages of the book of Acts and believe that the children were excluded from participation in this established practice of baptism in the middle east, especially since most of them were Jewish and well understood the religious rite of circumcision for newborn males.

The list continues and includes some of the fundamentals of our Catholic Church most Catholics have never questioned, though perhaps also did not fully appreciate. The **Pope**, the **Sacraments**, the **Sacramental Priesthood**, **Confirmation**, **Last Rites**, and more all became stones in a wall that stood up against my efforts to dismantle with impotent arguments.

As you might suspect, the greatest obstacle in my journey to understand the teachings of the Catholic Church also became the greatest gift—the **Eucharist**. I heard one apologist make the strong assertion that if the Eucharist is *not* what we believe it to be, then we are guilty of grave idolatry. But if the Eucharist is the true Body and Blood, Soul and Divinity of the Second Person of the Holy Trinity, then how can we do anything less than fall to our knees in worship of this Sacred Gift of Grace given to us in the Blessed Sacrament.

Questions to Consider

1. After reading this chapter about some of the challenges faced in making such a significant shift in views about Christianity and the Church, would you say that the theological or the interpersonal challenges are more difficult to overcome? Explain.

2. Have you experienced any push back in the practice of your own faith from members of your family? How have you dealt with it?

3. What would your response have been when my father made his strong comment about whether I believed the Eucharist to be the true Body and Blood of Jesus Christ?

4. From your experience with non-Catholic Christians, what are some of their challenges with the teachings and practices of our Catholic faith?

CHAPTER SIX

The Psychology of Conversion

After receiving my Master of Arts in Old Testament studies in 1981 and working in the local church setting as a member of the ministerial staff for six years, I was keenly aware of the need for practical help at the personal level as people struggle with depression, anxiety, interpersonal distress, marital conflict and much more. Perhaps providential, at that same time we were seeing several new graduate programs around the country emerging that were early attempts to integrate a sound Evangelical Christian worldview with psychological principles and practices. In 1983 I began my graduate work in Psychology and earned my Master of Arts in Counseling Psychology in 1989 and eventually my Ph.D. in Human Services in 2006. Since 1990 I have been working in the field as a licensed therapist in psychiatric hospitals, outpatient clinics and private practice settings and continue to provide professional services to this day.

It has been a rewarding career for me as I have been privileged to work with people through their suffering, teach in a major university graduate program, and provide the necessary clinical supervision for interns and residents to enter the field. Perhaps it goes without saying that our culture has been greatly influenced by the field of Psychology, which has not always been a good thing, given the liberal nature of the field that leans toward a highly secular-humanistic worldview.

What I was not prepared for in my journey into the Catholic Church were the psychological issues and challenges I would face. My respect and appreciation for the scholarly apologists who have paved the way for us to see the historical truth found in the Church is immense and I expected this would be sufficient to fuel my decision, but I would soon discover another formidable challenge—my psyche. That may sound too ethereal for some and too abstract to be credible for others, but it is real. For over thirty years I have worked with this hidden part of the human person. If we fail to recognize its presence and how powerful it can be we may fail to give people in search of our faith the means and resources needed to overcome the subtle psychological barriers and take those final steps into conversion.

All of us have had those frustrating conversations with someone over religious, political, cultural or any other potentially controversial issue and you think you're making progress in influencing him to consider your point of view, only to have him take a cognitive 180 and say something like, *"Well, I hear what you're saying, but I could never do that."* What happened? I thought we were almost there and then, out of nowhere, he just shifted into a resistant position. Here's what probably happened—your arguments were too convincing, too good and you were getting too close to influence them to take the next step. Then a part of his mind started thinking, *"Wow, I never thought about it this way. This sounds like it might be true. But if I accept it as truth, then I'm compelled to act on it or otherwise experience a great deal of confusion. And if I did act on this truth, I can only imagine what my wife would think...what my parents would think...what my friends would think. This is going to really be costly. And if I don't act on it...I'm going to be paralyzed by this dissonance. I need to shut this down and do it now!"* And out comes a rather illogical and ill-timed response that leaves you bewildered and speechless. That, my friend, is a psychological barrier you have just triggered in the person. Maybe this is what happened to King Agrippa when St. Paul made his defense of the faith before him and the monarch responded, *"You will soon persuade me to play the Christian"* (Acts 26:28).

Let me share a few of the more common psychological issues that can prevent someone from taking the final step toward conversion, whether it be to Christianity or from one Christian faith tradition to another one that holds different doctrinal, liturgical, and moral teachings or interpretations of Scripture.

- **Family Loyalty** – How will my spouse, parents, and siblings deal with this decision? I feel guilty just entertaining the idea of making this change in my life.

- **Cognitive Dissonance** – How can I resolve the confusion I would have about my family, loved ones and friends who hold different beliefs?

- **Grief** – If I make this significant change now, how can I manage the grief I would experience over not making this decision much earlier in my life?

- **Loss** – If I take this huge step what will it cost me? I'm going to lose the respect of my family and friends, the familiarity of how I worship, and countless other unknown parts of my life.

- **Change** – All the changes that would happen in my life would be overwhelming. I feel more secure in doing and believing what I have always known.

These are some of the factors that emerge in the mind of someone who is contemplating ideas and facts that are contrary to what they have known, perhaps all their lives. Never underestimate how strong these psychological pulls can be for any of us. Think about the last time you were cleaning out your clothes closet. How hard can it be to sort through your shirts, blouses, pants, dresses, shoes, coats and all the accessories, throwing out or donating the items you no longer wear or need and better organizing the ones you choose to keep. Then what you thought would take a couple hours stretches out over days and eventually you abandon the whole effort in frustration, maybe putting few useless t-shirts into a box to drop off at the local Goodwill and stuffing everything else back in your closet for another day that may never come.

What happened? You came up hard against the psychological dimension. This shirt was what you wore on your first date with your wife. That pair of shoes reminds you of the ones your Dad used to wear. Your brother gave you that jacket when he outgrew it. You obsessed over getting that coat and couldn't wait to buy it when you'd saved up enough. Are you getting the idea? These are not unique to some, rather common to all. Much of the time these resistant thoughts don't seem logical or rational, but don't let that dissuade you into discounting their strength.

Be prepared to encounter this mysterious force when you are trying to convince someone to consider our Catholic faith. And keep in mind this is not coming from some bad or negative part of the person. We all find an elusive sense of security in the past, regardless how well it holds up against health or truth, because it was familiar. Think about it in your own life.

Questions to Consider

1. Were you surprised by what you read in this chapter? What was your reaction?

2. Recall a time in your life when you were faced with a serious life-changing decision. Perhaps it was a new job or a move to another part of the country or even a new season life like the *empty nest*. Take some time to reflect on how it affected you psychologically.

3. What do you consider to be the strongest psychological factors that may prevent an individual from accepting a convincing truth?

4. Recall a time when you were in dialogue with someone about your faith. Looking back on it now, after reading this chapter, can you identify any of the person's responses as having a psychological basis?

CHAPTER SEVEN

Brought Home Through Prayer

Well over two years into my journey I found myself conjuring up questions that took me into further study, investigation, dialogue, and analysis. It seemed I would never be able to find all the answers. Truth be known, maybe I was creating obstacles that would put off the seeming inevitability of my decision. As I have mentioned earlier, my personality is characterized by a strong desire to check every box and fill in every blank. There is a clear difference between being duly diligent in conducting a thorough review of the history, the facts, the teachings, and the overall theology of the Catholic Church before making such a critical decision and taking on the impossible task of resolving every issue and eliminating every doubt.

Marcus, whom you might recall was my mentor in this journey and eventually became my sponsor, was growing weary of the meetings wherein we would tackle the latest issue. He was always ready to either give a worthy defense or step back and do his own research to find the best answers to my relentless array of questions. I think he knew I was stalling and putting up roadblocks to slow down the pace and possibly abandon the trek altogether. Finally, he pulled out the strongest and most powerful tool in his spiritual arsenal—prayer.

There were so many encounters where we would drink multiple cups of java and rally back and forth around everything from theology, spirituality, ecclesiology to liturgy, the saints and Scripture, conversing for hours. The truth is I love those debates and always learn, grow, and am inspired by them, despite how deeply impacting they may be. Yet there must be a goal, otherwise these are just good conversations without a teleological end. Marcus had an objective. He was determined not to be discouraged or dissuaded from discipling me into the Church. One time he said to me, *"Tim, I don't want you standing outside the restaurant, studying the menu, but never enjoying the 'meal'."* I knew exactly what he was referring to in his Eucharistic metaphor and his sincere passion was clear and evident.

Now, over two years into this, he decided a change in his strategic course was necessary. Realizing my questions would never end he challenged me and he did it with a compassionate boldness. His recommendation—*"No more questions, Tim. No more books. No more debates. I want you to go before the Blessed Sacrament and pray. Just pray."* What could I say to that? How could I argue against such an obvious next step? I knew the power of prayer. In fact, as an Ordained Minister and serving on the weekends as the Interim Pastor of a small church on the northside of Indianapolis, I devoted time each day to prayer, led groups in prayer and preached of the efficacy of prayer on Sundays in my ministry. The leaders of that congregation were confused, frustrated, even angered by the evidence they were hearing of my disturbing journey into what they considered to be a wayward version of the Christian faith. That's why I would occasionally go to the nearest 24-hour Blessed Sacrament Chapel in the middle of the night, usually around 3:00 am. At the time I did not know this was a holy hour, but it certainly was sacred for me.

For my non-Catholic readers you may not be aware of what I mean when I speak of the Blessed Sacrament, so let me explain. Catholic theology informs us that the Bishops have always had the successive apostolic authority to confect the elements of bread and wine brought forth in the Mass into the changed substance of the *flesh* and *blood* of our Lord Jesus, known as the Eucharist (Greek for the *Good Gift*). This is the *meal*

Marcus was wanting me to enjoy someday as a Confirmed Catholic, fully embracing the truths of the Nicene Creed.

The Eucharist is the *Flesh* and *Blood*, the **Soul** and **Divinity** of the Second Person of the Holy Trinity and we can do nothing less

The Blessed Sacrament in a Monstrance

than bow before Him, giving him the pious adoration

He is due. As a Protestant and somewhere well into my journey, I came to a place where I believed it was indeed appropriate to kneel in worship. There was only one problem, to what would I kneel and give my adoration? There I was one Sunday morning in the middle of our worship service, compelled from deeply within to drop to my knees and yet stricken with an agonizing confusion at the same time. This catapulted me to an entirely new place in my theological understanding to acknowledge humbly that the Eucharist is worthy to be adored.

John Paul II was a strong proponent of Eucharistic Adoration[6], encouraging every Parish to establish an opportunity for Adoration around the clock every day of the week, believing as he did so well in the power of this prayerful practice. You see, each day of the year, with the single exception of Good Friday, Masses are celebrated worldwide and miraculously bread and wine are transubstantiated into the body and blood of our Lord Jesus Christ. After the distribution of the Eucharistic meal to the faithful the Priest will place the

---

[6] Eucharistic Adoration is **a Catholic devotion dating back to the early days of the Church**. It involves exposing a consecrated host, the Blessed Sacrament, allowing people to sit and pray in the Real Presence of Jesus Christ.

remaining confected[7] Hosts into the Tabernacle, usually purposely placed directly behind the Altar on which our Lord's sacrifice was re-presented in this beautiful Liturgy through the ministry of the Priest. In Eucharistic Adoration the Priest will reverently place a single consecrated Host into a Monstrance where it is then placed on an altar where it can be exposed to those who would desire to pray directly to our Savior. This is where my journey came to a sudden conclusion and rightly so.

This is a good place to share my favorite and possibly one of the most compelling moments in this walk of faith. Marcus and I were scheduled to meet at a set time, but he was running late. In my effort to be kind and sociable I asked what would become a fateful question launching this entire journey. **Where have you been?** He answered, **"Eucharistic Adoration"**. And I asked my second daring question of him, **"What's that?"**

Marcus' explanation of the practice of devotion to the Blessed Sacrament was compelling, yet I failed to grasp the full implication of his description. My

---

[7] *Confected* is the term used to designate when Holy Communion has been consecrated and is now the Sacrament of the Holy Eucharist.

response was to tell him a story about something that had happened recently in the Evangelical Church where I was serving as Interim Minister on the weekends. We had come to a place as leadership where we decided Communion (the Lord's Supper as we called it) would best be distributed through the practice known as **intinction** in which the recipient would take a piece of bread and dip it in the wine, thus receiving both elements. I went on to tell him about a dear older woman in our congregation who offered to make the communion bread for the services each week and it was delicious. One Sunday following the service I made my way out of the sanctuary and down the hall to the office I was using on the weekends, only to walk past the Youth Minister's office and find three young teens chowing down on the remaining communion bread from the service only minutes earlier. I was appalled by their disregard for the sacred nature of the bread they were eating, and I expected upon sharing this anecdote with Marcus he would realize how similar our faiths were.

That did not happen. Instead, he responded almost without so much as a hesitation with a pointed question of me, *"What do you care? You don't believe it's the actual Body and Blood of Christ anyway?"* What was I to say to that? He was right! I did not believe the substance of the bread and wine were in any actual way transformed, just that this was a Sacred Memorial act in which we reverently recalled the sacrifice our Lord made on Calvary as he instructed of us. Marcus did not miss the stunned look on my face, not to mention my awkward silence, which prompted him to give me the tape series by Dr. Hahn when next we saw each other as I shared back in chapter four.

Now, well over a year later, he came to a point of perhaps frustration with my resistance and strongly admonished me to stop with the questions, the books, the discussions, encouraging me instead to just spend time in Eucharistic Adoration. I knew deep within it would take me down an off ramp from this journey that would likely culminate in my conversion. I suspect Marcus knew it too. And it did indeed.

At the risk of sounding a bit preachy, is there someone in your life, possibly a spouse, a son or daughter, a friend who you have been trying to persuade to return to the Catholic Church and practice of their faith? Use your own sanctified judgment always, but never doubt the power of prayer and trust that God will put the right people in his life at the right time. That is what

God did for me and I didn't see it coming. But when it came I could do nothing less than follow His graceful leading.

Questions to Consider

1. Does your church practice weekly observance of Holy Communion, assuming you are not Catholic? What is your understanding of the practice? If not, did you ever wonder why it is not observed at your church?

2. If you had been in my shoes when Marcus challenged me about my disbelief in Communion what would you have said?

3. Could you ever see yourself pushing a Christian from a different church to examine their beliefs as I was pushed? What might prevent you from doing so? Is it worth it to remain silent?

4. The Catholic Church tells us the Holy Eucharist is *"the source and summit of the Christian life"* What does that mean to you?

CHAPTER EIGHT

The Struggle to Belong

Easter Vigil 2003 at St. Simon the Apostle Catholic Church in Indianapolis, Indiana my wife and I were received into the Roman Catholic Church, a day I will never forget. Margie's path to the Church intersected with mine, yet we also found ourselves at odds on many an issue. Not to mention, she was even more content and fulfilled to serve and be a part of the church community where I was serving in ministry than I was, and as for me, the combination of my counseling work through the week and serving as the **Preaching Minister** on the weekends was profoundly satisfying. If this journey led me to a decision, it would mean the end of all that meant so much to both of us. It was through prayer, discussions with her Catholic friends, and a deep spiritual communion with God that brought my dear wife to join me on that beautiful evening in mid-April 2003 and receive the sign of the Cross.

Before my resignation, the preparation and delivery of sermons for the congregation I loved was getting increasingly difficult. As you might expect, my studies in the Early Church writings and countless apologetic volumes written in defense of the Catholic Church were influencing my theology and my teaching. In fact, my final sermon I gave a sermon entitled

Gracepoint Church of Christ in Fishers, Indiana where Tim served as Senior Pastor.

Have a Mary Christmas in which I made a case for the perpetual virginity of our Lord's Mother.

In our church denomination we had men who served in the voted office of Elder. The term *Elder* is derived from the Greek word found several times in the New Testament *presbuteros*. Some translations use the Anglicized word *presbyter* rather than translating the term. The denominational founders who dated back to the early nineteenth century saw this office as synonymous with the *overseer* in the New Testament, particularly St. Paul's writings. The latter term is a translation of the Greek word *episkopos* which can be translated as *overseer* and as *bishop*, also an Anglicized version of the original word.

I recall one of our Elders Meetings attended also by the Ministers, including the *Worship Minister*, the Youth Minister and me, serving as the Senior Teaching Minister. One of the agenda items for the meeting was the question of whether women could serve as Elders. We were given the instruction by the Chairman to take the following month and give ourselves to a study of the New Testament as preparation for a discussion about the issue in the next meeting. Thinking to myself, *this is how the early Church arrived at its doctrine?* and I knew from my studies nothing could be further from the truth. Doctrinal creeds about every-thing from Christology to Soteriology[8] to Ecclesiol-ogy[9] were handed down as part of an authoritative Apostolic record to be observed without question. We, on the other hand, were about to have a discussion amongst the six to ten men and risk changing all of that. I then asked myself another series of questions—*Who am I to make these claims of truth? We say we are Biblically based in all we do and yet are we making decisions based on the truth of the Bible or our own flawed interpretation of the truth of Scripture?* The men were not altogether pleased when I came to the next meeting armed with a defense of a Biblical theology of the church resembling remarkably that of the Catholic Church. I even shared an apostolic constitution from Pope John Paul (now Pope St. John Paul II), *Ordinatio Sacerdotalis,* translated to English—**Priestly Ordination** issued in 1994 in which he defended the Church's position requiring "the reservation of priestly ordination to men alone" and added

---

[8] Catholic soteriology (salvation theology) is rooted in Apostolic Tradition and Scripture and says that it is only by God's grace that one is saved.

[9] Ecclesiology is the theological study of the Catholic Church, its nature and organization.

that "the Church has no authority whatsoever to con-
fer priestly ordination on women".

The matter of *authority* became central in my quest
to understand. Where can I find the seat of authority,
the reliable source of truth upon which I could place
my confident trust and obedience. Eventually I had to
confess my determination to posit all authority in the
Holy Bible was, in practice, an exercise in self authority. It was my interpretation of Scripture that I had always defended, supported by my chosen leaders of a
religious movement driven by good men with a devout
desire to practice only what could be found in the
pages between Matthew and Revelation. But I could no
longer ascribe to this interpretive approach that
claimed to be correctly Biblical in all matters. We
were, as the Chairman's encouragement to study and
discuss revealed, an authority unto ourselves.

A shocking realization crashed down upon me in
that moment—I don't belong. No longer could I hold
to the arguments of our movement. A commonly
heard axiom we used, *No creed but the Bible*, did not
stand up against the tens of thousands of splinter
groups among Evangelical Christianity who would
each declare their interpretation the right one, not just
on seeming trivial matters of the faith, but on the

critical doctrines like baptism, sanctification, justification and so many more.

The one paradoxical truth I could no longer deny was that I did not hold all truth, nor could I possibly study sufficiently to know all the relevant truths of Christianity. The fulness of truth lay within the historic Catholic Church or to quote **Lumen Gentium**:

> This Church constituted and organized in the world as a society, subsists in the Catholic Church, which is governed by the successor of Peter and by the bishops in communion with him, although many elements of sanctification and of truth are found outside of its visible structure. These elements, as gifts belonging to the Church of Christ, are forces impelling toward catholic unity (Lumen Gentium, 8)[10].

Cardinal Joseph Ratzinger, later elected Pope Benedict XVI, clarified the term subsists—*"The Council wants to tell us that the Church of Jesus Christ as a concrete subject in the present world can be encountered in the Catholic Church"*.[11] This is what I had now come to

---

[10] Pope Paul VI, 1965

[11] Joseph Ratzinger, "L'ecclesiologia della Costituzione *Lumen Gentium"* in R. Fisichella (ed.), *Il Concillio Vaticano II: Receione e attualita* alla luce del Giubileo (Cinisello B. 2000), 79.

believe, and I could do nothing less than act on that belief.

Saturday evening, April 19, 2003, I received our Lord and Savior under the veil of bread and wine transubstantiated into the Body and Blood, Soul and Divinity, of the Lamb of God who takes away the sins of the world. My life would never be the same. The "sabbatical" I was requested to take by the church leaders where I had been serving for over three years had eventuated to a resignation. My ordination as a Minister in the Christian Church no longer meant more than a memorable ceremony resembling true vocational Holy Orders. Most of our friends were confused and bewildered by what we were doing. Some were clear and direct in their disagreement with our spiritual path, but most were passively silent and just faded from what had been a shared fellowship of mutual encouragement.

These feelings of being marginalized were countered by my excitement over how I presumed the Church would welcome us and my anticipation of invitation after invitation to share my journey, teach the faith, and serve faithfully in lay ministry. Perhaps some prominent Catholic Seminary would snatch me up and ask me to join their faculty to teach Scripture studies or Psychology. Parishes across the country would hear of my conversion, wanting me to come and give a Parish Mission. How would my schedule accommodate all the upcoming demands? Or so I thought.

My favorite Christmas movie of all time is **White Christmas** with Bing Crosby, Rosemary Clooney, Danny Kay and Vera-Ellen. In the scene where Crosby's character performs a song on a television show to invite the General's former battalion to join him in a surprise reception, he sings a song with these lyrics,

> When the war was over, there were jobs galore for the G.I. Josephs who were in the war. But for generals things were not so grand. And it isn't hard to understand.
>
> What can you do with a general when he stops being a general? Oh, what can you do with a general who retires?
>
> Who's got a job for a general when he stops being a general? They all get a job, but a general no one hires.[12]

Change the word "general" for "pastor" or "minister" and those lyrics express my sentiment rather well. This may sound like self-pity. It is not. Just grief over

---

[12] White Christmas movie (1954)

giving up a work that meant the world to me to come into a faith community that did not know what to do with me. The years to follow my conversion were marked by a sense of loss and loneliness. Eventually my professional expertise proved useful to the Marital Tribunal and one person who knew of my story shared it with the Director of the Ecclesial Lay Ministry Program of the Diocese who asked me if I would like to teach some Scripture courses. Leading those ten or

St. Simon Catholic Church where Tim and Margie were Confirmed Easter Vigil, 2003.

twelve adult students enrolled in the ELM program was very rewarding, despite it being quite the contrast with my expectations. Later, at the request of the Vicar General, I was involved in the teaching formation of the men preparing for Ordination in the Permanent Diaconate.

The Parish Priests where we attended were less inviting of me to offer my services. Like the retired general in the song, they seemed either confused how I could offer anything to the Parish or were just too busy with their own pastoral duties to follow up on their earlier expressions of interest in my offering to serve. At one point I took it upon myself to offer an adult study after Mass in the Fellowship Center to discuss the Readings for the Liturgy. The five or six regulars who attended were generous with their appreciation, but it was clearly not anything like my Evangelical days of teaching and preaching to hundreds of interested listeners.

The dissonant feeling of isolation was only intensified by my encounter with Catholic laypeople and even some Priests who were disinterested in my story or even questioned it altogether. One associate on the staff came up to me after giving my testimony and told me in naïve honesty she didn't understand why I left my Protestant Church, adding, *"Isn't that your way of worshiping?"* What had I done? Where was the Church I had studied about? Did it only exist in theory and historic idealism? Little did I realize I had embarked upon another part of my spiritual journey.

Questions to Consider

1. This question is meant to be prompting, not judgmental. When was the last time you lingered after Mass, observing those who may have seemed a bit confused in the Liturgy and even going so far as to approach them to introduce yourself and perhaps inquire if they're new to the Parish? Who knows but you just might happen upon an inquirer like I once was in the Mass.

2. St. Paul admonishes us that he gave leaders in the Church *"for the equipping of the saints for the work of ministry"*. How does that strike you after reading this chapter?

3. What are you doing to serve in the Church? We are all gifted and called to serve in some capacity. What are your gifts and where is your calling?

4. How would you have responded to the staff member who asked me why I left the Protestant Church?

CHAPTER NINE

A Lay Ministry

That last chapter may have left you wondering if I regret my conversion to the Catholic Church. Nothing could be further from the truth. It just took me by surprise that I had to carve out my place in the service of the faith after becoming Catholic. Yet as a therapist I appreciate that every religious community has a cultural distinctive. Some elements of that culture may be good and reasonable, while others may be problematic and contribute to a dysfunctional status quo. The culture of the Catholic

Church tends to be more closed than open, bearing in mind that I'm using that **broad brush** again. One way to Illustrate this observation would be to attend your local mega-non-denominational evangelical church on any Sunday morning and count how many times you are greeted with a warm smile and a welcoming comment. Then compare that experience to last Sunday's Mass where many attenders hustled in within five to ten minutes of the opening processional. And how do you account for all those open spaces in the middle of a pew with polarized participants sitting on the aisles, unwilling to give up their prized possession of a seat so near the exit. These are characteristics of a **closed system** that doesn't have too many **open doors** or they are not clearly identifiable.

Long before our decision to enter the Rite of Christian Initiation (RCIA) at our local parish, I began attending Mass on Sunday mornings. It's one thing to read about Liturgy and a whole other to participate actively in the Liturgy. I struggled, and that struggle was fairly evident to anyone who might have noticed me fumbling about trying to find where we were in the Scriptures or where I could locate a copy of the Nicene

Creed. Prior to our involvement in RCIA[13], no one showed me how to use a Pew Missal. Everyone seemed to be minding their own liturgical business and I was left to figure it out on my own. One Sunday at Mass, however, when I stepped forward to receive a Blessing from the Priest, I was in tears. Father Bob noticed my distress and approached me after Mass, asking me how I was and if I needed anything. His sensitivity was a much-needed answer to my prayers for someone to reach out from the Parish and offer help and accompaniment, which he did. Perhaps though, we as the laity need to consider how such small acts of kindness may be part of the evangelization effort and not relinquish the work of sharing the faith to the Clergy. Father Bob would be the Priest to offer Margie and me our first taste of the Holy Eucharist, and also to baptize our son, Brian, who was six years old at the time. In honor of our request, Father performed the baptism by immersion, in keeping with our tradition.[14]

---

[13] Rite of Christian Initiation for Adults is the process used in Catholic Parishes to welcome new converts, their baptism and Confirmation usually taking place each year on Holy Saturday during Easter Vigil.

[14] Immersion was the baptismal form of the early Christians and still a preferred form of the Sacrament as it aptly portrays the death, burial, and Resurrection of our Lord, into Whom we are being baptized. (See Romans 6:4)

Over time I learned the liturgical **rules** and parochial **customs**. But I can't help but wonder if my journey would have been abbreviated and less challenging had there been more outgoing, friendly, and welcoming Catholics to reach out and draw us in, as is more typical of the average evangelical community. There have been some reliable studies conducted that **friendship** Is the strongest and most compelling factor for someone to affiliate with a religious community, not **theology**. For me it **was** theology that motivated me to press on. For most I dare say it may not be enough. We must help the inquiring individual take their next step into our Catholic faith.

Let me add here that once we were enrolled in RCIA and became regular in attendance at the Mass in our local Parish, there were several people who reached out to us. Alice, Mark, Aaron, Angie, Ashley, Kerry, Matt, Randy, Linda, Joe, Mollie, Adam, Will, Kristen, John, Melissa, Ming, Lori, and many others became our friends and companions as Margie and I made our journey into the Catholic Church. Through involvement in Retreats, small groups, and Parish events, we were integrated into the local family of our Lord at St. Simon.

One more comment on this point—as much as I desired and prayed for another Evangelical, (other than my wife who was my greatest support and companion in this journey), to agree with me on what I was discovering and join me in this walk of faith, I now think God was saying to me, *"Tim, this is your journey and you must make it on your own! I am here for you. Margie has opened her heart to this conversion. Now, trust me!"* After making the decision to go forward with RCIA and enter the Catholic Church then others from our Evangelical community began to follow. Our good friends, Brian and Kimlarie found themselves convicted to enter prayer about returning to the Church for him and being Confirmed for Kimlarie. She was a close companion for Margie for the duration of her journey and the four of us remain strong partners in the Catholic faith.

This may perhaps be an overly critical portrayal of the Catholic community and I think it important to point out a central difference in the worship practices of the Catholic and Evangelical worlds. The non-denominational Christian Churches hold their worship services out as the primary means of evangelization of the non-believer and unchurched. From the moment a person drives into the parking lot of their facilities they will encounter a concerted and usually beautifully sincere effort to give that guest an encounter that is warm, welcoming, and full of Christ's love. This is sometimes referred to as "consumer Christianity" wherein the visitor is given an experience that will lead to a return visit, much like the local coffee shop that welcomes you with a warm greeting upon entry. In fact, in the last decade we have also seen another phenomenon among these Christian Churches where they build in a coffee shop into their foyer or welcoming area that resembles and likely competes well with any local java restaurant. And if you're wondering whether the worshiper can take their beverage into the place of worship, the answer is yes. Why? Because the objective is comfort and welcome that will give the attender a felt experience of being safely at home in this place.

The differences with the Catholic Mass are enormous and must be appreciated if we are to understand this seeming disparity of charity in the community. I want to point out three vital distinctions in the two worship paradigms. First, the Mass is a liturgical experience for the confirmed Christian who has given full personal affirmation of the doctrines stated clearly in the Nicene Creed. This explains why the early con-firmands were dismissed after the Liturgy of the Word, the first part of the Holy Mass, until they had been baptized, confirmed in the faith and fully assimi-lated into their Catholic communities.

Second, because of this first key reality the Mass is not to be seen or used as a tool for evangelism. That is not, nor ever has been, its purpose or place. Evangeli-

The Eucharistic Prayer during the high point of the Mass.

zation is what we do when we leave the place of wor-ship, having been filled with the teachings from the Bible and the Sacred Meal of the Eucharist[15]. We live our lives with the theological virtues of faith, hope and

---

[15] The Eucharistic Prayer, which begins when the priest extends his arms and says, *"The Lord be with you...life up your hearts...let us give thanks to the Lord our God..."* is the heart of the Mass.

love on display for the world to witness and be drawn toward.

A third point regards the very definition of worship. Most non-denominational Christians will define worship as singing, prayer, Bible teaching and fellowship. Worship in the Catholic sense is defined by one word—*sacrifice*. Through the Ordination of a Bishop and the reception of the Priesthood, the Celebrant presides over a liturgy in which the readings from the Scripture all lead to a heavenly meal of the Body and Blood, Soul and Divinity, of the Lord Jesus Christ as His holy sacrifice is *re-presented* on the Altar in the presence of the confirmed believers participating in devoted response and reception[16].

The Catholic Church has long been accused of being *exclusive* as it places such requirements of belief, devotion, and piety upon those who would receive the Lord in the Sacrifice of the Mass. Truth be known the critical observation is valid. The privilege of eating of the Body and Blood of the Second Person of the Holy Trinity is a sacred gift that only the truly believing and

---

[16] Christ's bloody sacrifice on the cross of Calvary will never be repeated as that sacrifice was perfect and efficacious. The Mass is a participation in this one heavenly offering.

devoted Christian who understands the meaning and is in a place of humble purity should receive. St. Paul clearly exhorts us, *"For anyone who eats and drinks without discerning the body, eats and drinks judgment on himself"* (1 Corinthians 11:29).

Perhaps the evangelical Christian community, to extend the grace and love of God to the world, has lost sight of and respectful appreciation for the sacredness of worship and the God-given requirements to be a part of a family whose beliefs and practices are indeed distinct from and *exclusive* of other beliefs and practices. In a culture that casts a severe judgment on any such religious group that dare distinguish itself apart from the world the Catholic Church stands as one of the few institutions that is unquestionably religious, undeniably exclusive, and yet indisputably available to anyone who desires to learn, submit, and be transformed into the likeness of Jesus through the Sacramental graces the Church provides.

As I conclude this chapter it bears noting the distinction that must always be appreciated between the proper theology of Christ's Church and the visible expression of it in the local Parishes in which we serve. There will always be a margin of difference that can lead us to disheartenment or disillusionment at how poorly we live out the faith, whether as laity or even clergy. But the Church is a Divine-Human Institution and though the Holy Spirit is always at work in His Providential oversight of the Body of Christ, we in our concupiscent[17] human condition may still fail to fully comply with that Godly direction. The result will be that the Catholic Church we see in our communities may bear little comparison to the rich ecclesial picture we see in the Scriptures, the writings of the Early Fathers, and the work of modern-day apologists for the Church. But, this is why we must let that gap in our current reality draw us ever closer to God and long for the Heavenly Courts where we will worship Him in the great Mass of the Ages which John calls *The Lamb's Supper*.

---

[17] Concupiscence is understood as an effect of original sin that remains after baptism. The waters of baptism cleanse us of original sin itself, but concupiscence remains as a lingering effect. The Catechism of the Catholic Church teaches that "certain temporal consequences of sin remain in the baptized, such as suffering, illness, death…as well as an inclination to sin that Tradition calls concupiscence" (No.1264). Perhaps more simply put, it explains our tendency to veer off course and how it is impossible to go straight without constant correction.

Questions to Consider

1. Think about recent experiences at the Mass. Can you recall seeing anyone who seemed a bit out of place? If not, imagine such a scene. What if the person was sitting in the pew directly in front of you and you can tell he seems to be there with a measure of curiosity? What would be an evangelistic action you could take after the final blessing?

2. Having answered that first question now consider what might prevent you from taking that action? Fear? Awkwardness? Embarrassment? What stands in your way?

3. Do you leave Mass with a greater sense of felt urgency to share the faith with others? How could you increase your motivation to tell others about why you are a Catholic?

4. Were you surprised by anything you read in this chapter? Comment on it here.

CHAPTER ELEVEN

Historical Foundations

I have always been enthralled with history. The best novels, in my humble opinion, are historically based and written by an author who did his best to create a drama within a past reality that was true to form. We all have a connection to our ancestors. They live on in our memories of them and through our faith we believe they are alive even beyond those fading recollections.

One of my all-time favorite movies is the remake of **The Jazz Singer** with Neil Diamond starring along with Lawrence Olivier as his Jewish father. In one dramatic scene where Oliver's character is scolding his Cantor son for betraying his religious roots in favor of becoming a pop singer star, the father gives a powerful lecture to Diamond who plays the part of an Assistant Cantor in their Synagogue:

> "There are some things is more important not to change! Our people were killed for saying a prayer a certain way. We owe it to them to keep on singing it their way. You can't change what has always been! That's how you know where you stand...who you are and where you come from. *And if you don't know where you come from, how do you know where you're going?*"[18]

That last line is what I find so penetrating and convicting. As a Protestant Evangelical I was not concerned much at all with my roots, at least not before the 18th century. Yet I knew better than to accept such illogic and the deprecation of history. My years of concentrated study in the history of the Hebrew people from Abraham to Mary and Joseph provided me the typological backdrop for properly understanding

---

[18] The Jazz Singer movie, 1980

Christianity and interpreting the New Testament within that teleological[19] history.

A three-volume series by William Jurgens entitled *The Faith of the Early Fathers*[20] will  sufficiently make the case by providing historical passages from the Christian writings of the Pre-Nicene and Nicene eras. Take, as an example on the matter of the ecclesial structure of the early church, a letter of St. Ignatius of Antioch dated c. 110. That is within a mere twenty years after the death of the apostle John.

"Take care to do all things in harmony with God, with the bishop presiding in the place of God and with the presbyters in the place of the council of the Apostles, and with the deacons, who are most dear to me, entrusted with the business of Jesus Christ, who was

---

[19] The term **teleology** comes from a Greek word that refers to direction and focus. That is, history is not a random cycling of events, rather always to be understood as on a trajectory governed providentially by our Creator God. This teleological paradigm of time itself does not end with the birth of Jesus, rather extends throughout the period of the Church to this present day and will continue through all eternity to come.

[20] Providing a wide array of early church writings translated into English, *Faith of the Early Fathers* offers excerpts of critical theological developments in the first seven centuries of Christian history.

with the Father from the beginning and is at last made manifest."[21]

This one paragraph is enough to challenge the inconsistency within the current state of Christendom regarding the structure of leadership roles and offices within the Church that is so diversified and at odds among the countless denominations, most of whom would assert they are following an Apostolic, Biblical model. Could Ignatius have erred from the given design in just two decades? Perhaps, but not likely.

Many people have a passion to discover their family history and invest money and countless hours to online platforms like *ancestry.com* to learn of their past. It only makes sense that we would want to know as much as possible about our origins. Should we be any the less motivated to know how our family of faith originated and developed through the centuries? The texts are available to us, the most vital ones stemming back to those first six centuries following Jesus' establishment of his Church with the Apostles before ascending into Heaven.

But let me give you an important word of caution—be aware that once you open those historical pages you

---

[21] LETTER TO THE MAGNESIANS [*ca. A.D.* 110]

may not be able to turn back from the destination where it may lead you.

Questions to Consider

1. How much do you know about the history of Christianity? What do you think you might discover if you were to read those early writings discussed briefly in this chapter?

2. Now take the opposing position for a moment. How would you argue against the place of history in support of the historical Catholic Church that has survived over two millennia?

CHAPTER TWELVE

An Unchanging Voice of Truth for a Changing World

S ome days I read the news and am astonished, even shocked, at how unrecognizable this culture is to me. I don't think I'm just being nostalgic when I say that the secular world in which we now live has challenged countless elements of the Judeo-Christian faith and its core tenets. Consider just a few:

- The meaning of marriage as a lifelong covenant relationship between a man and a woman.

- The Divine creation of mankind in the Image of God as male and female.

- The sanctity of life from conception to natural death.

- Even the universal application of the moral law as found In the Ten Commandments.

No longer should these realities that have their roots in antiquity and the Scriptures be taken for granted. Even worse, Bible-believing Christians are usually judged for being too conservative and thought to be self-righteous.

At each celebration of the Mass we recite the familiar words of the Nicene Creed, a belief statement that emerged out of the First Church Council of Nicaea in the fourth century. In the recitation of those strong words, we reaffirm our confident agreement in the truths of the Christian faith. The last section states clearly that there is *one, holy, catholic, and apostolic Church*. Four distinctives that identify the integrity of Christ's family, the Church. Let's look briefly at each one.

First, it is noteworthy that these descriptors are not arbitrary, rather expressions that come from the nature of God Himself. The *oneness* of the Church is a reflection of the indissoluble nature of the Godhead, Three-in-One of the same substance, though three Persons in the Father, the Son, and the Holy Spirit. His Body, the Church, can no more be a fragmented entity comprised of variant forms, practices, and doctrinal beliefs, than the Three Persons of the Trinity be at odds with each other.

Second, remember that the Church is called to be a *holy* community. That truth flows logically from its Divine origins in its Holy Spouse who provides the graces to achieve that Holiness through the Sacraments. The Sacraments can only make sense fully when recognized in the context of their God-given nature. When we fail to see that connection, we will be tempted to view them as modifiable practices that can be conformed to cultural appetites without regard to their historic meaning.

Third, the term *Catholic* is the word that causes many Protestants to shriek in rejection of any such relationship to the Catholic Church against which their 16th century reformers protested. Etymologically, the term emerges from the Greek and can be translated as *universal*. Cultures may differ and countries have their own histories, but the Church founded by our Lord in A.D. 30 is to be universal throughout the world, calling all to step into the saving ark that will deliver us from sin and death.

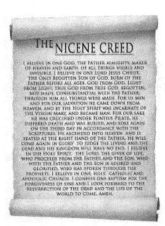

And last, the Church is *apostolic*. This is such a remarkable quality when properly understood. It affirms that the Bishops of the Catholic Church today are inextricably linked to a line of ordained successors dating back to the original twelve Apostles called and ordained by Jesus Christ. The practice of ordination is not left up to an individual or even a local Christian community. Instead, it is the Sacramental expression of our Lord's continued leadership over the Church that is purposed with guardianship of the true faith delivered to those original twelve apostles who were called to follow Jesus during his earthly ministry and carry out his mission after his Ascension into heaven where he continues to make intercession for us.

As our world moves further and further away from the core truths and values found in Christianity, we should be even more compelled to know what that theological **plumbline** is and hold to those Divine standards firmly. St. Paul warned his younger disciple Timothy with these words that ring ever relevant to our own 21st century condition – *"Proclaim the word; be persistent whether it is convenient or inconvenient; convince, reprimand, encourage through all patience and teaching".*[22] I am no longer an Ordained Minister, but there is no less obligation on me to respond to that admonition than Bishops and Priests. As baptized Christians we have a calling on our lives to carry out the ministry of evangelization and discipleship. There is much work to do. Just a few verses later, St. Paul went on to encourage his young disciple, Timothy, with the words—*"Fulfill your ministry!"*[23] May we all hear those words and take them to heart!

---

[22] 2 Timothy 4:2
[23] 2 Timothy 4:5

Questions to Consider

1. Regardless of your age, look back in time over your life and consider how the culture has changed in its perspective of right and wrong, morality, and even its understanding of truth itself. What do you notice?

2. Why do you think it is critical that the Church's voice is unchanged throughout time?

3. Can you think of an example or two of where the culture has shifted from a Christian society to a post or even anti-Christian one?

4. Take the issue of the *sanctity of life* as a good case for the consistent teaching of the Catholic Church throughout two millennia. Though not altogether popular in this world that wants sex without consequences, do you think the voice of the Church is being heard?

CHAPTER THIRTEEN

Psychological Benefits of Liturgy and Sacrament

T his might seem an odd topic to include in a book about one's conversion to the Catholic Church, but it resonates well with me as a psychotherapist. Although the instances were rare and typically viewed through a Christmas Eve news story covering the Mass in Rome or the Rites of the Triduum at Easter during Holy Week, I saw the accoutrements of liturgy as unnecessary, pretentious, and out of line with what I believed was the simple message of Jesus. Why all the fuss of such trappings that seemed to only draw the focus onto the person leading, rather than the Person of Jesus Christ?

Then I started thinking about a wedding ceremony and how the bride and groom customarily adorn themselves with special garments, how there are trimmings of beauty placed in the sanctuary, and how *ritual-like*

Tim and Margie when he received his Ph.D. in 2006.

the entire experience is from the processional to the exchange of vows and the giving of rings. Another example that crossed my mind are the graduation ceremonies, from high school to college and especially graduate universities. When I received my Masters' diplomas and was awarded my Doctorate, all of us from the teaching staff to the students graduating, were wearing regalia with color coded markings to distinguish in symbolic fashion the various disciplines of education. Having a hood placed over my head on those occasions when I received a graduate degree was filled with rich symbolism. The ceremony would not have been the same were it not for the trappings.

So why would I look with such disdain at the vestments, the vessels, the aesthetics, and the rituals of worship? Remembering my days at Englewood Christian Church, I recalled the Elders[24], often led by my father who was the Chairman of the Eldership Board, processing into the sanctuary at the opening hymn, taking their places in the two formal wood chairs placed on either side of the Communion table with the words etched on the front – *Do this in Remembrance of Me*. These memories stayed with me over the years as I witnessed the all but complete transformation of worship from a formal, ritualized pattern of meaningful acts, to an informal place filled with chairs where there had once been pews, music stands and mics where there had once been a pulpit, video screens where there had been cloth drapes of various seasonal colors, a drum set that would make Phil Collins drool with envy where there had once been a baptismal font.

Please don't misunderstand my comments as being against contemporary Christian music or good

---

[24] As previously noted in chapter 8, the term Elder is one of the translations of the Greek word *presbuteros*, more often transliterated into the English term *presbyter*.

preaching. These are important practices that can enliven us in our faith and inform us in how to live faithfully as followers of Jesus. However, these emotionally charged times of singing with all the instruments, lighting effects, and sometimes even smoke are not liturgy. It is a bit curious though, when I think about the smoke and how the use of incense in the liturgy is so foreign and misunderstood by Evangelicals. I also knew very well as a Pastor, that we were devising these services either on our own or with a small group of well-intentioned musicians with no regard for the historical roots of the practices we so arbitrarily abandoned and replaced with modern ones more pleasing to the senses.

You may be asking, where is the psychology in all of this you first spoke of in this chapter? I would point to two aspects of worship that are deeply psychological in their nature, though that was not the original intent. The first is how these familiar practices provide us a deep experience of security. The second is how they become engrained into our inner worlds as a second nature way to give our adoration to God. Let's look at these two areas briefly.

The word *familiar* originates from the same word from which we get the term *family*. I cannot help but think of the many couples I have counseled who had their first big arguments at the Christmas holidays when their *family traditions* clashed. As one researcher rightly noted, all marriages are cross-cultural relationships. And yet despite the variants in family customs there is more we have in common than what separates us. Think about it—most people eat three meals a day and use forks, spoons, knives, plates, and cups when doing so. We have beds to sleep in and do so at night, awakening in the morning, preparing for the day, showering, brushing our teeth and getting dressed. The point I'm trying to make is that we are routine creatures, accustomed to order in our worlds. Why then would we be surprised that religion is filled with routine, repeatable, predictable, and thereby consoling.

The second aspect of liturgy that has psychological benefit is the way in which our minds incorporate these rituals into our very nature. They become part of our identity and the manifestation of that identity is seen in religious actions, like dipping a finger into holy water and making the sign of the Cross, genuflecting before entering a pew, kneeling before the Blessed

Sacrament, and reciting the Lord's Prayer after hearing the Priest say those two opening words—*Our Father*.

In my work with clients dealing with depression and anxiety they often present with lives that are disordered and even chaotic. Getting up in the mornings can be the most difficult activity of their day. Caught up in confusion and cognitive rumination they struggle to make even the smallest of decisions—what to have for breakfast, whether to shower or not, what wear for the day, and on it goes. I often devote a session to putting order into their day, especially the way they begin the morning. By establishing rituals they will observe daily, they do not have to make these small decisions, rather they just follow the prescribed *script*, like a liturgy for the day. What is so amazing is how it can provide some relief and even give them a sense of fulfillment for completing such small tasks.

Don't get me wrong, sometimes it's nice to change it up and try something new. But we generally function better when there is consistency in our lives and order to our days. I wrote a book on marriage several years ago and called it *The Liturgy of Marriage* because we have found that couples experience improved relationships over time when they have predictable patterns. We all crave a certain number of similar experiences in our days, weeks, months, and years. It feels good to know that Spring follows Winter which follows Fall which follows Summer. 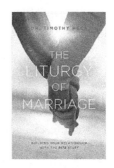 We delight in our holidays, in having turkey for Thanksgiving, in decorating for Christmas with those age-old lights and ornaments. Rituals, patterns, and liturgies are part of the fabric of our lives, serving as anchors, especially when the unexpected happens and life doesn't make sense. In those times it may be those daily routines that keep us from falling apart.

The structure I chose for the book finally came to me when I decided to use the elements of the Mass as a guide for explaining the vital ingredients for a godly marriage. And so, Part One is the Introductory Rite in which I talk about the beginnings of a marital relationship. Part Two explores the Liturgy of the Word, the second part of the Mass, and I illustrate how the Scriptures speak so poignantly to marriage. Finally, Part Three is the Liturgy of the Eucharist, wherein I attempt to challenge couples to make the Blessed Sacrament the center of their relationship and find the grace to overcome the difficulties we encounter in marriage and family life through the years.

Questions to Consider

1. What routines and rituals do you carry out on a daily, weekly, monthly, or annual basis? What would be the effect if you were told you couldn't carry these out anymore?

2. If you are Catholic, take some time to think about the many rituals you observe that are part of your faith practice. If you are an Evangelical or part of another faith tradition, do the same. Do you think these practices have psychological, as well as spiritual benefit to you?

3. Evangelicals do not usually use the term *liturgy* and yet if you attend a series of typical worship services at one of these churches you would probably notice a type of *liturgy* that might include an opening song, opening prayer, four or five praise songs, a thirty-minute sermon, an invitation hymn, and a closing prayer. Do you think such patterns constitute a form of liturgy for these faith communities?

4. The liturgy of the Mass has its root in the apostolic period of the Christian Church. What do you think about church leaders who take it upon themselves to tamper with ancient liturgies, modifying them to suit their preferences?

CHAPTER FOURTEEN

Illustrations

Occasionally I am asked to share my conversion story with children or teens. When presenting the reasons why I left the Evangelical world to become a Roman Catholic it seems to be easiest to understand when using an object lesson for illustrative purposes. My wife thought it might be helpful to include a few of these in my book explaining my spiritual and religious journey.

Let's Print Some Money

This one always gets the attention of an audience. In preparation for this talk I will make my own version of a twenty-dollar bill. The only problem is that instead of Andrew Jackson's picture I use Mickey Mouse. And rather than the Federal Reserve I like to call it My Personal Reserve. After adding a few unique bells and whistles I color it green and cut it to the same size as the real bill.

You can imagine the reactions when I tell the children I've come up with a new currency to buy stuff.

 It's fun to interact with them and more than a few of them have told me I'm going to get in real trouble if I try to use those fake bills. Then comes the big question—what makes these made up $20 bills different from the real thing? I might give them a hint and tell them the word begins with the letter "A". That's when they shout out, *"Authority!"* and they're exactly right. I don't have the

authority to print up my own currency. That authority belongs to the Federal Government.

My point—when the Protestant Reformers left the Catholic Church to establish their own *church*, their own priesthood, their own liturgy, their own canonical law, and much more, they did so without the **authority** of the Church that existed since 33 A.D. Of course, they had issues and many of them were valid, but just as we may have issues with those in political leadership, we do not have the option of disobedience and rejection of the governmental authority, and neither did the Reformers have the ecclesial authority to set up their own religious structures.

The Yolk's *On* You!

This one can be a bit messy, so *"don't try this at home, folks"*. The truth is your home may be just the place to pull this trick off. To start with you'll need at least a few eggs. That's right—eggs. Take a needle and poke a very tiny hole on the end of an egg. Then do the same thing to the other end. Place the bigger end of the egg up to your mouth and blow into the small opening you just made. Sounds ridiculous, I know, but what will happen when you blow is that the whites and yolk of the egg will leak its way out the other end. It takes a few minutes and a bit of hot air, but eventually you'll have a hollow egg. Repeat this as many times as you like, depending on how many **participants** you want to use when you do the presentation.

I bring an egg carton filled with all the hollow eggs,

but there is always one egg that has **not** been hollowed out and so is filled with egg white and yolk. In other words, it's the **real thing**. In this talk with the kids or teens I make the focus on the Eucharist and tell them that in my former church we also observed Communion. But the difference was that we thought it was just a memorial of the sacrificial death of our Lord Jesus

Christ on the cross. It meant a great deal to us as we observed the Lord's Supper in our weekly time of worship, but the bread was not really the Body of our Lord, just a regular piece of unleavened bread.

Now comes the fun part. I tell the kids that our communion bread looked just like the real thing, sort of like all these eggs. But it wasn't the true Eucharist, Body and Blood, Soul, and Divinity of the Second Person of the Trinity. And that's when I ask for my volunteers to come up and try a little experiment with me. I disclose to them how I emptied out all these eggs of their contents of egg white and yolk...all but one of these eggs. Without being able to touch them, only by looking at the eggs, then the kids must make a choice. A word of caution: Have a wet washcloth and towel on hand for this presentation.

One by one the kids make their choice and after the choice I have them turn and face the audience before I break the egg over the head of the person who made the choice. And you guessed it—at some point the real egg is discovered when the contents drip down the head of the good sport participant. And that is when you need the washcloth and towel.

The hopefully obvious point of the illustration is that another church's communion can look, taste, and seem like the real thing, but it is only in the Catholic Church that we have the confidence to know by faith that the Priest acting in union with the Bishop, who is the present-day representative of Apostolic authority, can we be assured this Eucharist is the real thing, the Body and Blood, Soul and Divinity of our Lord Jesus Christ.

All Menu—No Meal

One more example before I conclude. This one is simple. Create and print out a menu for a five-star restaurant they've never heard of and give it a spectacular name, like **The House of Heavenly Food**. Go to great lengths in describing how accurate the menu is, how it was composed centuries earlier by some very special chefs, and how it depicts the most delicious of meals ever tasted. Explain how it has been translated from an ancient language that no one now speaks, but through linguistic studies we can make clear sense of the ingredients for each of the items on this menu. Work it up as much as you like. Recommend to them that they memorize what is on the menu.

After a few minutes of playing it up, then you hit them with the one very important caveat—the restaurant never serves what is on the menu. Tell them in this restaurant people just come and read the menu, but they never have a meal. In fact, the people who are looking

forward to this restaurant opening will meet in small groups, share together in quite meaningful ways, and talk about their growing appetites for this meal yet to be served. Ask them how many times they would come back to this restaurant, knowing they never actually serve the meal being described.

This one always reminds me of the time my sponsor, Marcus, pleaded with me in his effort to bring me to accept the teachings of the Catholic Church and said passionately, ***"Tim, you've been studying the menu all your life. I want you to taste the Meal!"***

Questions to Consider

1. Suppose you were asked to explain your faith to a group of children and were going to use an object lesson in doing so. How would you do it?

2. If you are Catholic, how would you further distinguish the Catholic Church from the Protestant and Evangelical Churches in a way that the children can better comprehend?

3. Of the three illustrations provided in this chapter, is there one that stands out more meaningfully to you? Why?

4. Do you think we might overly complicate matters of faith and the Church? Jesus used parables to teach and found that effective with some, while falling on deaf ears with the more intellectually sophisticated. Do you think there are any applications to be recognized with his approach?

CHAPTER FIFTEEN

Concluding Thoughts

M y greatest concern in writing this book is that I would come across as condescending, or even worse, condemning of Christians in the Evangelical or mainstream world of the faith. I am forever grateful for the faith my parents held so dearly in their lives that compelled them to raise their children in the Christian faith. To be judgmental is not at all my intent in sharing this story of my own journey. There are many apologists who have defended the Christian faith and the Catholic Church far more eloquently than found in these pages. This effort was not meant to be a convincing argument for why one should consider Catholicism. But I do hope it has prompted you to at least consider what you do believe and even why you believe it. To this day I do not understand why the Holy Spirit considered me a receptive vessel to hear the fulness of the truth about the Church Jesus founded. Why I was gifted with the faith to accept these truths and participate in the Sacraments of the Catholic Church, I do not know. But I am grateful he opened my eyes and softened my heart, humbling me to become a student and learn from my teachers, both ancient and contemporary.

The stakes are higher than they have ever been. Our enemy, the Devil, seems to be gaining ground in this anti-Christian culture. When faced with questions, challenges, and even persecution for our Christian faith and Church allegiance we must be prepared, not only to defend what we believe, but to stand steadfast for that faith.

The final argument I want to put forward for my decision to enter the Catholic Church is the one found in my heart and soul, reinforced by coincidental, though I believe Providential, surprise encounters. Purely personal and subjective in nature, these experiences were powerful in bringing me through the process. I could tell you about the time I was in the Minneapolis Airport on my way back to Indianapolis and two people approached me. The backstory is that I was struggling with two key issues, one theological—the Blessed Virgin Mary, the other personal—my parents' faith and their faithfulness to their church. The second question was resolved when Gary, one of the Pastors at my parents' church, whom they highly respected came up to me and assured me of his continued love and support. The first question, about Mary, was resolved when a woman whom I had never met in my life approached me and gave me a book about Mary, saying to me, *"God told me I was to give this to you."* Both are personal experiences I had that convinced me.

Perhaps a year or so before our Conversion, Margie and I were invited to participate in the spiritual retreat, known as **The Walk to Emmaus**[25]. In those four days participants are assigned a table with four others and a small group leader. Little did I know I would be

---

[25] Curiously, **The Walk to Emmaus**, is a Protestant version of **Cursillo**, a spiritual retreat that has its origins in the Catholic Church of Spain. Dare I say, all good things come from Rome.

joining Dr. Chuck Dietzen, physician, and founder of the Timmy Foundation. Chuck had the honor a few years prior to visit Mother Theresa (now St. Teresa of Calcutta) and gave me a precious metal that had been touched by her[26]. Interestingly, someone in the church where I was serving gave Margie a video about a project sponsored by a Christian Ministry that was bringing children from third-world countries to the states for a cardiac surgery to repair a faulty valve. They were looking for families to host the child(ren) and parents during their stay here for the surgery and recovery period. We called and volunteered, but the need had been filled. But we were told by St. Vincent's Hospital, where the surgeries were being performed by surgeons who donated their services, that there were children in Haiti who also needed the same procedure and host families were needed. So, we volunteered and had the privilege of hosting two young children and their parents from Haiti for about six weeks. Guess what organization was responsible for the arrangement—the Timmy Foundation, of course.

---

[26] There are biblical accounts of people being healed of infirmities by touching something of or belonging to a godly person. See 2 Kings 13:21 and Acts 19:11-12.

Then there was the time when one of my friends who served as an Elder at Gracepoint Church where I was on staff came with me to Colorado for a skiing trip. On one of the lifts going up the mountain at Keystone we were joined by none other than a Priest who was more than thrilled to hear about my journey. What are the odds? Unfortunately, my friend was not as pleased as I was. Even more ironic was that we rode up with that same Priest a second time on the lift later that day.

Another example was when the representative for the company that handled our practice voicemail and paging service learned that I was looking into the Catholic Church and wanted to get coffee. During that conversation I mentioned Scott Hahn, whose books I had been reading. When I said his name, Phil, who had been a Presbyterian Pastor prior to his job at the time, said to me, *"Scott Hahn...I went to Gordon Conwell Seminary with a Scott Hahn. It couldn't be the same person."* The next day I received a call from Phil, and he was somewhat excited to tell me it was the same Scott Hahn. Phil had called Scott and he was happy to talk with me. I only had a few exchanges with Dr. Hahn, but they were intensely meaningful in my journey.

During our first conversation while giving my background I mentioned where I had attended Seminary in Cincinnati. Dr. Hahn quickly interrupted me and asked if I knew Rich Mullins. When I told him Rich was a fellow classmate during those years Scott nearly broke down in tears on the other end of the phone and disclosed to me that he was giving private instruction for Rich up to the day the singer was tragically killed in an auto accident September 19, 1997. You see, Rich, being the *Ragamuffin*[27] he was, always had an affinity for St. Francis and a leaning toward Catholicism. Dr. Hahn shared that Rich had plans to be received into the Church on October 4th of that year, the Feast Day of St. Francis of Assisi. That is why I chose St. Francis as my own Patron Saint when I entered the Catholic Church.

These are not going to convince anyone to explore the Catholic faith, but they played a huge part in my own conversion. Rich was compelled by *Liturgy* so much more than what he called *"the razzmatazz of modern worship"*. He once returned from church on a spiritual high, exclaiming *"Wow, I just took*

---

[27] Rich Mullins was a contemporary singer and songwriter whose story is now available in video format on a film entitled **Ragamuffin**.

Communion, and if Augustine were alive today, he would have had it with me. And maybe he was. And maybe he did." I can hear him saying this and it touches me deeply. Most of you reading this don't even know who Rich Mullins was, but you probably know some of his music, particularly his worship song, **"Awesome God,"** remains a favorite among Christians.

St. Augustine (354-430 AD) Bishop of Hippo

I faithfully attend Sunday Mass and try to go to Daily Mass whenever I can, but not as much as I should. Sometimes the music is poor, the homily is boring, and my fellow parishioners won't even slide down the pew to allow me a seat. It doesn't matter. The Liturgy of the Word and the Eucharist is transforming me like nothing else has ever done in my life. It shapes my very identity, connects me mysteriously with my loved ones who have gone before me in death, and renews my hope in the eternal destiny for which I long, to be with my Lord in the Heavenly Courts and give Him the adoration He is rightly deserving, the praise I owe Him, and bathe in his unfathomable Glory forever!

Selah![28]

---

[28] Scholars of the Scripture are not in agreement about how to translate this Hebrew term. Some say it means "praise" or "exalt". I had a Professor of Hebrew who preferred to translate this enigmatic word that appears frequently in the Psalms as *"think about it"*.

CHAPTER FIFTEEN

Epilogue

When asked if I miss being a Pastor, my response is always a heartfelt *"Absolutely!"* I was solidly convinced that God had called me as a minister of the Gospel of Jesus Christ. In fact, during a time of personal struggle while in Seminary I strongly considered abandoning that call and giving up my studies. A friend and fellow student, Mike, came to me out of bold love, using those words of the Apostle Paul I referenced previously and said to me, *"Tim, fulfill your ministry!"* I recommitted to my work and graduated a year later.

On the sad occasion of my first marriage[29] ending in crisis I attended an Evangelical Church service where I had never previously worshiped. My heart was overwhelmed with a grave sense of failure. Before the time of worship there was class where the speaker was discussing the topic—Reasons why we don't hear God speaking to us. Ironic. I had written my first thesis for my Masters in Old Testament Studies on that very topic. Anyone who has put in the time to research and compose such a piece of writing knows that the author becomes somewhat of an *expert* on the topic, or so I thought. His first point humbled me to my knees. He said, *"We often do not hear God speaking to us because of preconceived ideas of how He will speak to us"*. Wow! That one hit me right between the eyes. To be honest, I don't remember the other two points. This was more than enough to get my attention.

Next came a time of music, prayer, and meditation. I was a mess and my soul was crying out to God, *"Lord, I have failed you and I am not worthy to be a Minister."* It was then and there that I first heard the sweet

---

[29] The story of my marital failure is recounted in the book, **THE LITURGY OF MARRIAGE**, which I wrote, published in 2017 by Cradle Press.

melodies of an old worship song, *As the Deer*[30]. With tears streaming down my face someone tapped me on the shoulder. It was the Pastor of the church who wanted me to come to his office. Utterly confused and with no idea what was happening, I followed him, entered his office, and took a seat. He introduced me to a woman sitting at the table. *"Tim, this is Tamara, and she has had a word of knowledge about you this morning. She would like to share it with you."* Oh no, was my first thought, not some charismatic who thinks she heard from God?! Then it hit me. The message I had just heard about why we fail to hear God speaking to us. Could it be that he really did have a message for me? What did I have to lose? I listened cautiously.

Tamara was holding a small card in her hand and began to tell me what she had experienced earlier that morning. *"The Lord showed me a vision of you this morning when I was praying at my kitchen table. He told me you have been very discouraged in your faith. He said you are struggling greatly. And he wanted me to share a Scripture with you."* Tamara then read the parable of the Sower from Mark 4:1-9. Then she went on, *"Tim, you are the sower, but you have been sowing*

---

[30] Marty Nystrom, Composer

in your own strength, not His." As an arrogant self-sufficient young man, I was instantly convicted of the truth of the words on my life. But there was more and what she said next would bring me to a rush of agonizing, yet joy-filled, tears. It still does. She added, *"One more thing, Tim. God wants you to know that He has called you as a minister of the Gospel of Jesus Christ!"*

The Prayer Card given Tim from Tamara

"As the deer pants for streams of water, so my soul pants for you, my God. My soul thirsts for God, for the living God. When can I go and meet with God? My tears have been my food day and night, while people say to me all day long, 'Where is your God?'"[31]

Dissonance—dis-so-nance: a tension or clash resulting from the combination of two disharmonious or

---

[31] Psalm 42:1-3 (New International Version, 2011)

unsuitable elements. The word describes what I wrestled with on this journey of faith. To this day I remain solidly convinced of two truths: One, I was called as a Minister of the Gospel of Jesus Christ, and two, the Catholic Church is the Church founded by Jesus Christ in the first century. My response to this dilemma is to view my counseling, my teaching and speaking opportunities, and my writing as the manifestation of that ministry. It is not what I thought it would be, nor what I wanted it to be, but it is enough. It is my humble gift of service to God. I owe Him everything!

My friend, Claire Dwyer, in her book[32] about St. Elizabeth of the Trinity, recounts the story of how Elizabeth was an accomplished pianist before following her calling to enter religious life at the Carmel. *"For Elizabeth, music was not just an extension of prayer; it was prayer: love seeking expression."[33]* Yet, she had to sacrifice that part of her life to enter this new life where God had called her. I was again brought to tears when I first read Dwyer's commentary regarding the Saint's sacrifice—*"This sacrifice, like all sacrifices, is*

---

[32] THIS PRESENT PARADISE: A Spiritual Journey with St. Elizabeth of the Trinity, Dwyer, C., Sophia Institute Press.
[33] Dwyer, C., p.23

never wasted. God is glorified in our willingness to lay down even His own gifts at His feet."[34]

There is a spiritual refreshment in believing that God did give me my calling to the ministry and has also asked me to sacrifice that gift for the greater good of His glory. It eludes my understanding, but not my will. The loss surfaced for me just recently with some very good friends of ours with whom we have reconnected through their move from Indianapolis to Colorado Springs. They were members of Gracepoint, the church where I served as Pastor in the late 90s. Ken still says he thinks of me as his Pastor to this day. That sentiment was expressed when he asked me a few weeks before this writing if I would perform the wedding ceremony for his son later this summer. He probably had little idea the pain this would bring in my soul as I again faced the loss of my ministry and now must try and explain to these beautiful Christian friends why it would be illicit for me, as a layman, to function in the capacity of an Ordained member of the Clergy.

We are all called to lay down our lives, pick up our crosses, and follow Jesus, not looking back, rather rejoicing that we have been counted worthy to serve in

---

[34] Dwyer, C., p.23

His Kingdom, regardless the role or capacity. Thanks to teachers and apologists like Dr. Scott Hahn and countless others, many Protestant Pastors have taken that proverbial plunge into the waters of the Tiber to make their way to Rome and know the fullness of the truth in the Catholic Church. Please pray for them. It is a painful and costly journey. This was my journey of faith. Thanks be to God for bringing me through it!

"I am a sinner saved by the grace of God, undeserving of the love the Lord Jesus showed to me when He took my sins upon Himself and hung on that cross so that I can have the hope I would never have earned on my own. More flawed than gifted, foolish than wise, and drawn to comfort more than Holiness, I remain on this journey of faith until the day He calls me home to be with Him. This is my prayer! This is who I am."

Grace-fully,
Tim

BIBLIOGRAPHY

Boles, H. L. (1932). *Biographical sketches of gospel preachers.* Gospel Advocate Co.

Dwyer, C. (2020). *This present paradise.* Sophia Institute Press.

Hahn, S. (1993). *Rome sweet home: Our journey to Catholicism.* Ignatius Press.

Hahn, S. (2023). *St. Paul Center for Biblical Theology.* Scotthahn.com.

Hahn, S. (1999). *The Lamb's supper: The Mass as heaven on earth.* Doubleday.

Heck, T. (2017). *The liturgy of marriage: Building your relationship with the Rite stuff.* Cradle Press.

Jurgens, W. A. (Translator). (1979). *Faith of the early fathers: Three-volume set.* Liturgical Press.

New American Bible (Revised Edition). (1970). Good Will Publishers, Inc.

Newman, J. H. (2015). *An essay on the development of Christian doctrine, sixth edition.* University of Notre Dame Press.

Pope Paul VI. (1965). *Dogmatic Constitution on the Church – Lumen Gentium.* Libreria Editrice Vaticana.

Ragamuffin. (2014). David Leo.

The Holy Bible, *New International Version*. (2011). Grand Rapids: Zondervan Publishing House.

The Jazz Singer. (1980). Republic Pictures.

Timmy Global Health. (2023). Timmyglobalhealth.org.

U.S.C.C.B. (2019). *Catechism of the Catholic Church*. United States Catholic Conference of Bishops; 2nd edition.

Walk to Emmaus. (2023). *The upper room.* Upperroom.org/walktoemmaus.

White Christmas. (1954). Paramount Pictures.

"The Church exists for nothing else but to draw men into Christ, to make them little Christs. If they are not doing that, all the cathedrals, clergy, missions, sermons, even the Bible itself, are simply a waste of time. God became Man for no other purpose."

-C. S. Lewis

9 781088 096512